Instructor's Resource Manual

Teaching Strategies: A Guide to Better Instruction

Fifth Edition

Instructor's Resource Manual

Teaching Strategies: A Guide to Better Instruction

Fifth Edition

Donald C. Orlich
Robert J. Harder
Washington State University

Richard C. Callahan
Callahan Associates

Harry W. Gibson
Saint Martins College

Houghton Mifflin Company Boston New York

Sponsoring Editor: Loretta Wolozin
Associate Editor: Lisa Mafrici
Senior Project Editor: Carol Newman
Manufacturing Coordinator: Sally Culler
Marketing Manager: Pamela Laskey

Printed in the U.S.A.

ISBN: 0-395-87246-4

1 2 3 4 5 02 01 00 99 98

Contents

PART 2 INSTRUCTIONAL RESOURCES (Continued)

PART 2 INSTRUCTIONAL RESOURCES (Continued)

PART 2 INSTRUCTIONAL RESOURCES (Continued)

PART 2 INSTRUCTIONAL RESOURCES (Continued)

PART 3 OVERHEAD TRANSPARENCY MASTERS 79

Transparencies are Numbered Serially for Each Chapter on Pages 80-188

Preface

The *Instructor's Resource Manual* with ready-to-use attachments is designed to accompany *Teaching Strategies: A Guide to Better Instruction,* Fifth Edition, by Donald C. Orlich, Robert J. Harder, Richard C. Callahan, and Harry W. Gibson. This guide is organized to be user-friendly to the individual who is responsible for teaching the instructional methods course.

In Part 1, we present an overview of the manual, how to use the guide, and an extended discussion of an extensively tested qualitative evaluation method, simulated classroom lessons, an adaptation of micro-teaching. Two actual course syllabi are illustrated: One for a 12-week quarter, the other for a 15-week semester. Part 2 consists of the course resources, while Part 3 contains the reproducible black-line transparency masters that are keyed, respectively, to each textbook chapter.

The authors genuinely encourage your feedback about the organization and materials presented. It is your handy course helper—at least that is our intent.

Over the past years, we had much help in preparing the various instructors' manuals. We wish to acknowledge those colleagues—James B. Carroll, David Coffland, Deborah J. Handy, Cindy Rada, and Anne L. Remaley. A very special tribute goes to Sandra Tyacke, our long-time production assistant who prepared the many book-length manuscripts and this camera-ready copy.

PART 1

INTRODUCTION

Overview of Textbook and the Instructor's Resource Manual

Teaching Strategies: A Guide to Better Instruction, Fifth Edition, is organized into four major parts: Part One—A Framework for Instructional Decisions, Part Two—Fundamental Tools for Instructional Planning, Part Three—Instruction as a Dynamic Process in Classrooms, and Part Four—Assessing Your Students' Achievement and Your Professional Goals.

The Instructor's Resource Manual (IRM) is organized in a parallel manner, especially in Part 2. In Part 1, we discuss some strategies that we have used in teaching our general teaching methods courses and then illustrate two model course syllabi, one for the quarter system and one for the semester organization. The textbook can be used equally effectively in either time frame.

Part 2 of the IRM provides a series of chapter resources that include: (1) Overview of the Chapter, (2) Relevant Student Activities, (3) Topics for Class Discussions, (4) Focus Resources, (5) Student Evaluation Techniques, and (6) Overhead Transparency Masters Lists.

Part 3 of the IRM contains black line overhead transparency masters arranged in serial order by chapter.

Our rationale in designing the IRM is to help the busy instructor with a practical and useable guide that reflects how we have successfully taught our methods courses.

Using the Resource Guide

In this guide, you will find hints on how to plan and organize your own course. However, the various items presented here are designed to be altered and modified to meet your own instructional circumstances. Some of you will have field centers or professional development centers where your students blend actual teaching experiences with instructional methods while they are enrolled in relevant education courses. This structure requires that all persons involved in the teacher education program have an orientation to your methods of instruction course. Field-centered courses have one advantage in that your students are able to practice instructional techniques as they are learned in class.

There is a general movement in educational assessment to stress *performance.* Just what constitutes performance is not entirely clear. In many cases, the *performance* is to memorize or recall information, data, or concepts. In this IRM we provide examples of several assessment techniques by which to determine student competence. However, to evaluate teaching, one really needs to judge some kind of performance or teaching act. To this end, we devote the next section to a technique that we have used since at least 1968—*Simulated Classroom Lessons.*

Simulated Classroom Lessons

We now turn our attention to the topic of Simulated Classroom Lessons, an adaptation of microteaching, a technique that affords beginning teachers excellent opportunities to plan and rehearse a wide array of new instructional strategies. Our goal is to provide a rather easy-to-use interactive learning technique. Our textbook describe numerous teaching methods in which your students may develop and implement additional lessons so as to experience, rehearse, and experiment with various instructional techniques or methods.

What Is A Simulated Classroom Lesson?

A Simulated Classroom Lesson (SCL) is a scaled-down sample of teaching. It is essentially an opportunity for preservice or practicing teachers to develop and rehearse specific teaching skills with a small group of students (four to six peers or "real" students) by means of brief (six- to fifteen-minute) single-concept lessons. These teaching episodes are recorded on videotape for reviewing and analyzing very specific teaching processes. The SCL is a technique that allows your students to place incremental aspects of teaching under the microscope. More specifically, SCL is an empirically tested procedure that allows your students to do the following:

1. Rehearse a new technique, strategy, or procedure in a supportive environment.
2. Prepare and deliver a mini-lesson with reduced anxiety.
3. Test new ways to approach a topic or lesson.
4. Develop very specific delivery techniques such as introducing a topic, giving an assignment, or explaining an evaluation procedure.
5. Be evaluated by observers.
6. Gain immediate feedback of the teaching episode by viewing the video playback.
7. Risk little but gain much in valuable experience.
8. Subdivide complex teaching interactions into related elements.

Outside the classroom setting, SCL provides the closest simulation of teaching yet devised. As you prepare future educators, you will want them to strive for excellent, not merely satisfactory, performance. The goal is to support self-improvement. The Far West Educational Laboratory report shows that Simulated Classroom Lessons are powerful ways to change teaching behaviors (Borg et al. 1970). Janice Bertram Vaughn (1983) provided evidence that it did not matter whether college peers or students from the appropriate grade level made up the "simulated-class." The results are equally positive and beneficial.

The basic objective of SCL is the subdividing of multifaceted teaching acts into simpler components, so that the task of learning new instructional skills is more manageable. When prospective teachers engage in an SCL lesson, they focus on a specific aspect of teaching until they develop a satisfactory minimum competency of that skill. If you judge that a specific skill is not mastered, then schedule a reteach session to perfect it. The preservice teachers proceed to new skills after having achieved success with each preceding one.

Before assigning SCL, however, you need to consider the circumstances. First, not every topic, concept, or process automatically lends itself to every teaching method. Each concept needs to be analyzed carefully to determine whether or not it is appropriate for the assigned skill or for the specified time allotted to conduct the episode.

Second, in situations where it is not possible to obtain school-age students for the teaching sessions, a modified form of teaching may be used. For example, students enrolled in your education class may play the role of the school students. Also, because of a limited amount of class time, your reteach sessions may need to be kept to a minimum.

Cognitive *skills* (in the form of single-concept lessons) as well as *processes* may be perfected through SCL. The notion of single-concept lessons will be addressed later. But first we need to define what we mean by *processes* of instruction.

Instructional processes concern how one implements a specific teaching act. Some illustrations of processes that you may want to teach through the SCL technique include:

1. Introducing a new topic or concept.
2. Giving an assignment to a class.
3. Specifying how the students will be evaluated in the course.
4. Asking questions.
5. Conducting recitation sessions.
6. Tutoring an individual or small group.
7. Leading a discussion.
8. Practicing inquiry and problem-solving skills.
9. Summarizing student statements.
10. Closing a discussion or a class period.

The list is far from complete. You may think of many others. What is comforting to the learner (or prospective teacher) is that SCL allows one to rehearse a skill in "safety." It is a simulated form of teaching; the reality is there, but without the harsh realism of a classroom. With the SCL approach, you can isolate one tiny segment of the totality of teaching and rehearse it until the process is mastered. With this approach you have the opportunity to practice and master a skill before using it in a classroom.

Preparing for Simulated Classroom Lessons

A Simulated Classroom Lesson is not just "getting up front and teaching." The technique requires that you first prescribe carefully selected behaviors that you want practiced. As in "regular" daily lessons, the objective(s) must be carefully specified. Furthermore, you must establish a set of criteria by which you can judge how effectively your students are able to accomplish the desired skills, processes, or behaviors. The whole idea of SCL is to help improve teaching techniques through rehearsal, feedback, and evaluation.

Usually, SCL sessions last only six to ten minutes. To conduct SCL lessons, you will need a portable cassette recorder, one TV camera, and one microphone for a videocassette recorder (VCR) setup. This requires that you plan for at least one or two student technicians to operate the needed equipment. These should be students in your class. If a VCR setup is not available, use a cassette audiotape recorder, which will be nearly as effective.

Here is a "model" instructional objective for you to use in assigning a SCL.

Within the prescribed time limit and focusing on a prescribed process or teaching technique, teach a preselected concept to either a peer group of approximately five students or to five "real" students. The members of your simulated-class must achieve the performance objective as it is stated in the lesson plan, or you must accomplish the teaching process that you have specified in the plan.

For your students to accomplish this objective, they need to perform the following tasks for each SCL session.

1. Prepare a lesson plan using a suggested format. [We recommend an abbreviated version of the lesson-plan format found in Figure 4.2, Chapter 4, page 132.]
2. Make two copies of the lesson plan, one for your group leader and one for personal use while micro-teaching.
3. Teach the lesson to the student group within the time limit stipulated for the particular session.
4. Evaluate your student achievement by the use of a stated performance rubric and a specific evaluation device.
5. Critique in writing, by using an evaluation instrument, the teaching of the other students in the group. [Each small group should provide an immediate oral critique following each mini-lesson, plus yours, the instructor.]
6. Use a critique checklist or other evaluation criteria to aid in planning (see Figure IRM-1). Each individual lesson is to be critiqued after viewing and listening to the recording of the teaching.
7. Reteach the lesson, time permitting, to master the new technique.

Deciding on Simulated Classroom Lesson Content and Lesson-Plan Format

A critical point that you will need to stress to students as they prepare lessons is that they must learn how to *narrow the topic.* The purpose of SCL is not to demonstrate everything there is to know about effective instruction; rather, it is to focus on one aspect of the teaching process at a time. To accomplish this, stress selecting a single subconcept from the discipline of choice and develop a lesson aimed at helping micro-session students learn this concept in the short span of six to ten minutes.

Once your students have selected a single concept as the basis for their SCL lessons, the next step is to develop a *limited number* of performance objectives (perhaps only one). That is, students need to determine what behavior the "simulated-student" is to manifest in relation to the concept and to what extent he or she is expected to recall, recognize, or apply the concept.

We suggest that you follow the organizational format for lesson planning described in Chapter Four. Instead of using the format *in toto,* however, make careful "editing" decisions so that the resulting plan will be manageable within the limits of the setting. For example, you may not have enough time to allow for extensive "student practice." Although the planning procedures recommended previously will be generally applicable, they may need to be abbreviated to fit your particular objective(s) and circumstances. The ultimate criterion of a plan's effectiveness is: *Does it work during the actual implementation of the lesson?*

Simulated Classroom Lesson Planning Checklist

Since SCL entails much preparation (just as does systematic teaching), the checklist in Table IRM-1 is provided to assist you and the students in this important planning process.

Table IRM-1 Simulated Classroom Lesson Planning Checklist

	Activities	Check When Completed
1.	Student entry level known.	________
2.	Unit title, instructional goal/unit objective, and performance objective(s) properly written.	________
3.	Focus on a *single* concept.	________
4.	Rationale clearly stated.	________
5.	Content determined.	________
6.	Instructional procedures specified.	________
7.	SCL session evaluation or critique form developed.	________
8.	Audiovisual materials and special instructional items prepared.	________
9.	Two copies (original for instructor, copy for self) of lesson plan completed.	________
10.	Lesson delivered and peer evaluations given.	________
11.	Tape replayed.	________
12.	Self-critique conducted.	________
13.	Decision made about whether to reteach.	________

Simulated Classroom Lesson Feedback

Once your students have completed their lessons and have received immediate verbal and written feedback from their "students," they will be ready for what may be the most significant aspect of the technique—self-evaluation. The replay of an SCL session has great potential value in helping to identify strengths and weaknesses in the use of specific teaching approaches and strategies. The playback (learner feedback) is aimed toward helping students become the best possible teacher. The replay of SCL gives insights into how they appear, sound, and interact with their students.

In the interest of effectiveness and efficiency, your students should view the video recording as soon as possible after the actual SCL session—preferably immediately, but certainly no later than twenty-four hours after they have taught the lesson.

While observing the replay of SCL sessions, you will find it helpful to use an evaluation form with appropriate criteria for judging the effectiveness of individual teaching skills. The SCL evaluation form in Figure IRM-1 may help you design similar evaluative instruments to assess SCL lessons.

What kind of impact does SCL have on prospective teachers? Walberg reports an effect size of 0.55 on its use with preservice teacher candidates. That means it is an important technology to use in practicing and perfecting specific teaching acts or behaviors. Teachers in the field also benefit greatly from Simulated Classroom Lessons, where it shows an effect size of 0.90 for learning specific instructional strategies (see Walberg, 1991, pp. 60–61).

In the next section, we present two somewhat abbreviated course syllabi or frameworks by which to design a methods of instruction course covering either one quarter or one semester. These are authentic syllabi, for they are in use. Both complete syllabi contain rather extensive reading lists for students. These are omitted here since lists tend to change rather frequently. However, outside readings are encouraged since they provide students with supporting or alternative ideas to those found in the textbook.

Figure IRM-1. A Sample SCL Evaluation Form

Name of SCL Teacher ______________________
General Comments ______________________

I. Lesson Plan
Unit and Instructional Goal ______________________
Objective ______________________
Rationale ______________________
Focus on Single Key Concept ______________________
Distinction Between Content and Procedures ______________________
Sequencing of Lesson ______________________
Criterion Measures Specified ______________________

II. Management and Delivery ______________________
Focusing Event ______________________
Teacher-Student Eye Contact ______________________
Pacing of Lesson ______________________
Teacher Verbal Behaviors ______________________
Teacher Nonverbal Behaviors ______________________
Lesson Closure ______________________
Use of Materials______________________

III. Evaluation (knowing that the objective was reached) ______________________
Teacher and Students Know Whether Objectives Were Reached______________________
General Comments ______________________

References

Borg, W. R., et al. *The Mini-Course: A Simulated Classroom Lessons Approach to Teacher's Education.* Beverly Hills, CA: Macmillan Educational Services, 1970.

Vaughn, J. B. *A Comparison of Peer Teaching and Child Teaching in Preservice Teacher Acquisition of Enthusiasm, Praise, Probing, and Questioning Behaviors.* Ph.D. Diss., University of Cincinnati, 1983.

Walberg, H. J. "Productive Teaching and Instruction: Assessing the Knowledge Base." In *Effective Teaching: Current Research.* H. C. Waxman and H. J. Walberg, Eds. Berkeley, CA: McCutchan, 1991.

Syllabus for a 12-Week Quarter

Course Name: **Teaching: Curriculum, Methods, and Materials**

Section: **EDCS-311, Section 4 5-Credit Course**

Meeting Time: **M-T-W-Th-F 12:00 Noon to 12:50 p.m., Michaelsen Hall Room 209**

Instructor: **Gerald R. Brong, Ed.D.***

Course Description

Teaching: Curriculum, Methods, and Materials is designed to assist preservice teachers as they develop teaching skills in applying knowledge related to:

- Principles of designing courses of study, curricular integration, instruction, delivering presentation, and guiding student activities in programs resulting in learning for the students.
- Essential learnings, behavioral expectations for students, assessment, evaluation, bench marking, and procedures for implementing quality in education. Processes of continuous improvement and portfolio assessment will be introduced.
- Procedures for actively assuming responsibilities as a decision-making teacher.
- Multiple roles of a teacher in the diverse systems of education, classroom, and community, and among the professional associations of educators.
- Procedures for curricular development and the selection of content.
- Management of the classroom, student reports, and discipline.

EDCS-311 is specific to teaching and learning activities in the elementary, middle, and secondary school levels. Content will be applicable to public and private systems of education, though the emphasis will be on public systems.

Primary Content Areas

Core concept areas to be explored in *Teaching: Curriculum, Methods, and Materials* include but are not limited to:

- Quality principles applied to teaching, learning, and systems of education.
- Essential learnings and related curricular developments.
- Student testing, assessment, and evaluation related to program quality and results.
- Community resources as assets for learning and teaching.
- Laws, system structure, regulation, funding, and facilitation of public education.
- Process assessment used by teachers to guide the management of teaching.
- Selection of resources for use in teaching and in support of learning.
- Instructional methodologies and teaching styles.
- Classroom management and discipline integrated into a school's programming.

---

* Reprinted with permission of Gerald R. Brong.

A major emphasis of *Teaching: Curriculum, Methods, and Materials* will be teacher decision making. A primary orientation of the course will be development of knowledge, insights, and skills necessary to make and implement decisions resulting in quality teaching and appropriate learnings. EDCS-311.04 is an applications-based course.

Objectives for the Learners

Participants in EDCS-311.04 will:

- Create lesson plans appropriate to a learner group.
- Define topics/concepts/skills to be learned.
- Facilitate group learning activities by serving as "teacher" in EDCS-311.04.
- Participate in group research and decision making.
- Produce and use behavioral goals and measurable objectives.
- Demonstrate an understanding of mandated educational requirements.
- Manage class-course activities for a student group.
- Create and administer assessment/evaluation procedures.
- Establish marking/grading systems for students.
- Reflect on and apply prior and current learnings as a teacher in training.
- Use the Essential Academic Learning Requirements in the design of a curriculum, series of lessons, and assessment.
- Create evaluation systems for the purpose of measuring and reporting effectiveness of presentations, including demonstration lessons, offered by peers in the class.
- Select resources to be used in a teaching-learning situation. Included will be assessment of quality, costs, effectiveness, and availability of the resource.
- Develop an integrated teaching unit. Present the unit to a group of peers and justify content, pedagogy, processes of assessment, and evaluation of learner outcomes.
- Demonstrate a variety of behavior management and discipline techniques.
- Develop a personal philosophy of education. Present the philosophy to a peer group. Determine the relevance of the philosophy to the diverse systems of education in the State of Washington and the United States of America.

Required Textbook

Teaching Strategies: A Guide to Better Instruction (5th Edition) by Orlich, Harder, Callahan, and Gibson, ©1998 Boston, Houghton Mifflin Company.

Accept the Challenge

Influencing the learning of another person is almost as important as influencing your own learning. Life and the quality of life depend on learning. In our complex society it is the teacher in our diverse systems of education who, as a professional, has declared, "I accept the responsibility to influence the learning of others."

EDCS-311 directly confronts responsibilities of teaching, explores the skills necessary to be a teacher, and builds a person's intellectual capabilities in making decisions about teaching. Teachers are decision makers. As decision makers teachers influence the lives of others. Consider the number of lives you will influence as a teacher. Be ready.

Assignments, Projects, Grades

Based on advance planning, planning subject to change, the following assignments, projects, and criteria will relate to the course grade.

Attendance/Participation/Contribution/Professionalism	100 points
Three Unannounced Quizzes (50 points each)	150 points
Final Comprehensive Examination	250 points
Lessons and Teaching Demonstrations	300 points
Reflective Writing—Course Research Paper	200 points
Total for Course and All Activities	**1,000 points**

Tentative Grade Scale

A Range	900 to 1,000 points
B Range	800 to 899 points
C Range	700 to 799 points
D Range	600 to 699 points

Suggested Course Notebook Log

It is suggested that participants keep a "log" of course activities and reflections on the activities, readings, and discussions in the course. News items, ideas, Internet material, notes on text readings, etc., should be placed in this notebook. The notebook will be a primary reference resource used in the class.

Program Overview and Unit Topics—Tentative Schedule

Following are curricular units for EDCS-311.04, *Teaching: Curriculum, Methods, and Materials* as offered in winter quarter. The dates suggested and sequence may change as necessary for meeting learner and teacher needs, capturing opportunities, and accommodating unanticipated changes that become necessary. The goal for EDCS-311.04 is to assist you as you work to become successful as a teacher. It's hard work, but rewarding work. Accept the challenge. Earn, and enjoy, the rewards.

The preliminary and tentative schedule for your section of EDCS-311 is:

Unit #1—Teachers, Decisions, Schools, and Students—Weeks 1 and 2

- Review of Educational Foundations in the United States of America and the state.
- Student in Classrooms—From 4 to 84—Lifelong Learning
- Alternative Futures for Systems of Education and Schools

Unit #2—Learnings, Outcomes, Standards, and Quality—Weeks 3 and 4

- Essential Learnings
- Standards and Assessment

Unit #3—Design of Instruction: Where to Go and How to Get There—Weeks 5 and 6

- Processes of Planning and Implementation
- Objectives to Guide and as Benchmarks for Measurements
- Your Curriculum, Your Course of Study or Theirs

Unit #4—Delivery of Instruction: Facilitation of Learning—Weeks 7–10
- Classroom Management and Personal/Professional Management
- Communication, Diversity, Quality Assurance, and Quality Teaching and Learning
- Community-Based Education Using Community Resources
- School to Work and Community-Based Programming for Learners
- Assessment of Product and Process

Unit #5—Becoming a Teacher—Week 11
- Lifelong Learning—A Teacher's Responsibility
- Academic and Career Opportunities for Teachers—Be Thinking Now for Alternative Futures
- Reflections on Becoming a Teacher, Readiness to Teach, and the Immediate Future

Final Examination (Final Challenge) Week—Week 12

Syllabus for a 15-Week Semester

Course Name:	**Teaching in Secondary Schools**
Meeting Time:	**M, W, F, 11:10 am to Noon**
Section:	**1**
Instructor:	**Donald C. Orlich**

Introduction

"Teaching in Secondary Schools," T & L 303, is a basic general instructional methods course that is oriented to the needs of aspiring grades 4–12 teachers. The goal of the course is to provide a series of learning experiences to illustrate "multimethodology."

The course is organized around a relevant set of basic themes:

1. Schools and their settings
2. Teachers as decision makers
3. Tested techniques for organizing instruction
4. Classroom environments
5. Lesson designs
6. Questioning techniques
7. Discussion-leading models
8. Thinking skills inquiry and problem solving
9. Multicultural concerns
10. Assessment of learning
11. Lifelong learning

Each activity is grounded in the notion of preparing practitioners who will know the best practices of their field and who can evaluate the utility of any suggested teaching technique. Our model is dynamic, for as the research base changes, new knowledge is incorporated into the class.

The required textbook for the course is: D. C. Orlich, R. J. Harder, R. Callahan, and H. W. Gibson, *Teaching Strategies: A Guide to Better Instruction,* 5th Edition, Boston: Houghton Mifflin Company, 1998.

A series of required readings will be circulated separately.

General

It is very important that you read all assignments before they are discussed in class. Therefore, all readings not marked "Begin" must be completed prior to the next class. There may be surprise quizzes on the readings so check your schedule to remain current. Readings listed as "Optional" are given to provide you with in-depth treatments of the subject being covered. **ALWAYS BRING YOUR BOOK TO CLASS.** Attendance will be taken and is considered in the determination of final grades. Assignments submitted late are subject to a penalty involving a reduced grade. Lesson plans for Simulated Classroom Lessons (SCL) are due in advance as specified below. This document presents the class schedule for the semester. Special attention should be given to the Simulated Classroom

Sessions since attendance is mandatory during these important course requirements. **BRING VIDEOCASSETTES TO CLASS WHEN DOING SCL.**

In-Class Activity	*Preparation for Class*
Week 1	
1. Introduction and Overview 2. Schooling as an Institution 3. Orientation to Chapter 2 4. ERIC and CIJE	1. Begin Chapter 1 in Text 2. Begin *A Nation at Risk* 3. Begin Reading Chapter 2 4. Complete *A Nation at Risk* 5. Select your abstract article
Week 2	
1. Abstract #1, Due 2. Teaching and Decision Making 3. Goals, Standards, and Taxonomy	1. Complete Reading Chapter 2 2. Outside reading on reserve "The Changing Nature of the Disadvantaged Population . . ." 3. Begin Chapter 3 4. Abstract #1 Due Topics: Goals, OBE, Standards, Mastery Learning
Week 3	
Note: You will begin the T & L 303 Portfolio this week. Details will be announced in class.	
1. Test #1 (Chapters 1 and 2) 2. Discuss Chapter 3 3. Rationale, Objective, Evaluation 4. Lesson Planning 5. Planning for SCL 6. Discuss Direct Instruction Model 7. Bring one objective for SLC #1 8. Discuss Chapter 4 9. Review SLC Objectives	1. Finish reading Chapter 3 2. Begin reading Chapter 4 3. Read paper on reserve: "Twelve Middle-School Teachers' Planning" by D. S. Brown 4. Examine the formats for lesson plans. 5. Review model lesson on reserve. 6. Bring a written statement of your proposed objective for SCL. 7. Buy VCR tape needed for SCL #1 8. Practice your SCL lesson at home. 9. All lesson plans due for SCL #1
Week 4	
1. SCL #1 Locations to be posted. Bring 2 (two) sets of lesson plans, student materials, and VCR tape.	1. Begin reading Chapter 5

Week 5

1. Discuss instructional design and basic concepts.
2. Discuss Chapter 5 sequencing.
3. Task analysis.
4. Ausubel's model.
5. Brain and hemisphericity
6. Learning styles

1. Read Chapter 5
2. Begin Chapter 7
3. Reading on reserve, B. Bloom "Learning for Mastery"
4. Review topic about "Kaplan Matrix" in Chapter 4
5. Do a task analysis
6. Review "Seven Intelligences" and Learning Styles.

Week 6

1. Introduce unit plan construction (final course project)
2. Wrap-up of Chapters 3, 4, 5
3. Discuss required readings for Chapters 3, 4, 5
4. Test #2 (Chapters 3, 4, 5)

1. Review Chapter 5
2. Unit plans will be a continuous activity
3. Begin search for article about the use of questioning as an instructional tool

Week 7

1. Begin discussion of questioning as an instructional technique.
2. Discussion of Chapter 7
3. Review of Chapter 7

1. Complete Chapter 7
2. Begin reading papers on reserve
3. Select topic for SCL #2 (from text) and rough out lesson plan

Week 8

1. Questioning
2. Prepare for SCL #2
3. SCL #2. Locations to be announced.
4. Submit lesson plans (2 copies)

1. Chapter 7
2. Have lesson plan ready.
3. Post SCL schedule
4. Same equipment as in SCL #1
5. <u>All lesson plans due</u> for SCL #2

Week 9

1. SCL #2 continued.

1. Bring your own VCR tapes
2. 2 copies of lesson plan
3. Practice
4. Read Chapter 6
5. Be working on <u>Unit Plan</u>

Week 10

1. Classroom Management Principles and Practices

1. Orientation only, as you take a course on classroom management
2. Complete Chapter 6
3. Begin Chapter 8

Week 11

1. Introduction to discussion as an instructional tool
2. Rationale of discussions
3. Discussion Technique
4. Discussion techniques, applications

1. Finish reading Chapter 8
2. Chapter 8
3. Select article for abstract
4. Review for Test #3

Week 12

1. Complete work on discussion
2. Review for Test #3
3. Test #3 (Chapters 6, 7, 8)
4. Begin discussion about "Inquiry"

1. Begin Reading Chapter 9
2. Read papers on reserve

Week 13

1. Discussion of Inquiry Processes
2. Uses of inquiry in all classes
3. Relationship of inquiry to critical thinking
4. Introduce diverse and inclusionary aspects of instruction

1. Begin reading Chapter 10
2. Begin two readings on reserve
3. Abstract #3 is due
4. Orientation only, as you are required to take a course on the topic

Week 14

1. Diversity and inclusionary aspects of teaching
2. Introduction to Assessment

1. Read reserve paper by J. Banks
2. Complete Chapters 11 and 12 in text
3. Begin search for abstract #4
4. Brief review only, as you will take a course on the topic

Week 15

1. Complete Assessment
2. Lifelong Learning
3. SCL #3
4. Wrap-up and Course Critique
5. Test #4 will be the Final Exam: Times to be announced when scheduled. The final will cover Chapters 9, 10, 11, 12

1. Chapter 12
2. Same equipment as in SCL #2
3. VCR tape at correct spot
4. Location(s) to be announced
5. Abstract #4 due
6. Hand in Unit Plans and Portfolios on last day of class

GRADING SCHEDULE

Tests	31%	Maximum	Your Score
Test #1	Goals and Objectives	100	
Test #2	School Clientele, Decision-Making	100	
Test #3	Questioning, Discussion	100	
Test #4	Cooperative Learning, Diversity, Assessment, Master Teacher	200	500
Simulated Classroom Lessons	25%		
SCL #1	Teaching to an Objective	50	
SCL #2	Questioning	150	
SCL #3	Inquiry, Discussion, or Cooperative Learning	200	400
Papers	25%		
Abstract #1	Outcome-Based Education/ Instructional Planning	100	
Abstract #2	Questioning	100	
Abstract #3	Inquiry	100	
Abstract #4	Cooperative Learning	100	400
Complementary Assignments	19%		
Unit Plan and Portfolio		200	
Affective Measures (Miscellaneous Assignments/Pop Quizzes/ Attendance)		100	300
TOTAL	100%		1,600

1. If your written or oral work is of poor quality, we reserve the right to reduce your final grade to a D or F and recommend either supplementary course work or deselection from teacher education.
2. Approximate grading percentages and cumulative scores:

Grade	Percentage	Cumulative Score
A	93+	1488 and Higher
A-	90–92	1440–1487
B+	87–89	1392–1439
B	83–86	1328–1391
B-	79–82	1264–1327
C+	76–78	1216–1263
C	73–75	1168–1215
C-	70–72	1120–1167
D	66–69	1056–1119
F	65	1040 or Lower

EVALUATION SCALE FOR SIMULATED CLASSROOM LESSON #1

Instructions: Rate the teacher on each of the following items by circling the appropriate level of the scale.

	Superior		Adequate		Needs Work
1. Introduction was appropriate, motivating	5	4	3	2	1
2. Purpose of lesson was clear	5	4	3	2	1
3. Lesson was logically organized	5	4	3	2	1
4. Explanation was clear	5	4	3	2	1
5. Evaluation indicated student understanding	5	4	3	2	1
6. Teacher and/or students summarized main points of lesson	5	4	3	2	1
7. Teacher used pauses to allow time for students to think	5	4	3	2	1
8. Lesson Plan Quality	15	12	9	6	3

Points Scored: __________
(Maximum is 50)

Comments:

Simulated Classroom Lessons Evaluation—Second SCL **8–12 Minutes**

Name of SCL Teacher ______________________________ Topic ________________

Evaluator ______________________________

150 Points

Comments

I. LESSON PLAN
Clarity of Objective
Focus on Questioning
Objective Stated in Performance Terms (with all 3 parts)
Evaluation Specified—Formative or Summative
Sequencing Observable
Plan Developed for Questioning
0 5 10 15 20

II. MANAGEMENT
Orientation or Introduction
Interaction with Students
Pacing of Lesson
Poise: Enthusiasm
Appropriate Ending/Summary
0 5 10 15 20 25 30

III. QUESTIONING TECHNIQUE
Questions Showed Sequencing Strategy
Questioning Was Technically Correct
Questions Stated Positively
Wait Time I
Wait Time II
Questions Framed to Elicit Responses Other Than Yes or No
Appropriate Responses to Students
Questions Appropriate for Objectives
30 35 40 45 50 55 60 65 70 75 80

IV. EVALUATION
Plan Followed as Specified
Teacher/Student Performance Stated in Plan
Tasks Met as Stated in Objectives
0 5 10 15 20

GENERAL COMMENTS

Satisfactory __________
Unsatisfactory __________

Simulated Classroom Lesson Evaluation—Third SCL **10–15 Minutes**

Name of SCL Teacher ____________________

Evaluator ____________________ Topic ____________________

200 Points

Comments

I. LESSON PLAN
Stated Rationale and Goal
Clarity of Objective
Focus on Single Key Concept
Stated in Outcome Terms
Evaluation Specified
Explicit Instructional Technique Identified
Plan Developed for Technique
10 15 20 25 30 35 40

II. MANAGEMENT AND DELIVERY
Orientation or Introduction
Appropriate Materials Provided or Used
Positive Reinforcement to Students
Interaction with Students
Appropriate Ending/Summary
Rationale for Choice
Format Showed Development
Students Actively Involved
Responses to Students
Directions Appropriate for Topic
50 55 60 65 70 75 80 85 90 95 100 105 110 115 120

III. EVALUATION
Process Evaluation Plan Specified and Utilized
Teacher/Student Performed Tasks or Met Stated Objectives
10 15 20 25 30 35 40

GENERAL COMMENTS

Satisfactory __________
Unsatisfactory __________

Abstract Assignment

I. Purpose. The purpose of this assignment is to encourage each student to: (1) select and review a body of literature in the areas covered by the course, (2) become familiar with the breadth and variety of works representing the course areas, (3) increase proficiency in expressing ideas in written form clearly and concisely, and (4) become familiar with the professional journals and associations of respective disciplines.

II. The following elements should be included in the abstract.

1. What is the type and scope of the work? Is the work a review, a study, a theoretical work, or a statement of personal opinion or experience? What is the general content? How broad, narrow, or general is the work?
2. What is the article about? It may be important to state explicitly the limitations of a specific work. For example, a work may describe the advantages of a certain program yet only superficially deal with the disadvantages.
3. What is your assessment of the quality of the work? What are your conclusions? Although your own opinions can be included, a justification of the assessment should also be included.

III. Each assignment will be evaluated by the following criteria:

1. Development of the topic.
2. Accuracy in the citation format.
3. Mechanics of writing and spelling.
4. Overall format of the abstract.
5. Use of inclusionary language.

IV. The format for each abstract must meet the conditions listed below.

1. Provide a complete citation in one of the formats that follows. Note: Spacing is exact in the models that follow.

   Orlich, D. C. (1989). Education reforms: Mistakes, misconceptions, miscues. Phi Delta Kappan, 70, 512–517. (This is the APA style.)

   Orlich, Donald C. "Education Reforms: Mistakes, Misconceptions, Miscues." Phi Delta Kappan, 70 (1989), 512–517. (This is the Harbrace style for this assignment, however, please use APA style.)
2. The body of the abstract should be typed double-spaced.
3. Use one page only.
4. Write the abstract in the THIRD PERSON.

Part 2

Instructional Resources

1. The School and Its Clientele

Overview

Chapter 1 provides a brief introduction to the institution of schooling. The six parts can be viewed as a matrix showing the complex social and political interactions that take place in the public education arenas. The first part shows the largesse of public education and the contexts in which it operates.

Parts 2 and 3 examine how governmental and individual interactions occur in the schools, and the critical need for teachers to be aware of these circumstances. The summary of teachers' expectations on page 17 is not exactly an idealized "Our Miss Brooks."

Parts 4 and 5 illustrate the wide range of differences that one finds in any classroom. We simply introduce the concepts of diversity and inclusion, especially the orientation to the Americans with Disabilities Act (ADA). If our estimate is correct that 20% of children in the schools require some special educational interventions, then schooling and the delivery of quality service takes on an even greater challenge.

We close with a short presentation about the role that technology will play in the future classroom and how citizens do tend to view the schools rather favorably.

Relevant Student Activities

1. Using a Brainstorming approach, class members might be asked to recall the cultural symbols that they remember from their elementary, middle, and high school years.
2. A panel of students might be assembled to discuss the kind of school organization that exists in your state.
3. The Quadrilateral Dilemma on page 14 might be used as a stimulus for student position papers about the interaction of these institutions.
4. The table on page 24 and the discussion about PL 94-142 and the ADA might be used to stimulate a series of short research papers.
5. The PDK-Gallup Poll results for the past 10 years might be assigned to a research team for analysis and a later report to the class.

Topics for Class Discussion

1. To what extent is it the business of the school to be concerned about a child's socioeconomic status?
2. What traits did you observe in your "favorite" teachers? Compare them with the traits listed for novice teachers on page 18.
3. How can knowing about general traits of selected age groups help you to construct more developmentally appropriate instruction?
4. How do the concepts of diversity and inclusion interact in the classroom?
5. What are some methods for determining the public's perceptions of the jobs that are done in the schools?

Focus Resources

We suggest that the following paper be assigned as required reading because of its instructional implications.

Pallas, A. M., G. Natriello, and E. L. McDill. "The Changing Nature of the Disadvantaged Population: Current Dimensions and Future Trends." *Educational Researcher 18*(5) (1989):16–22.

Class members should be encouraged to browse the Web site of Phi Delta Kappa, publishers of *The Kappan,* one of the top-rated journals in education, for papers related to the themes presented in Chapter 1.

http://www.pdkintl.org/kappan/kappan.htm

Student Evaluation Techniques

Suggested Essay Questions

1. To what extent do intrinsic and extrinsic motivations affect individual decisions to become a teacher?
2. Contrast the role of the U.S. Department of Education with that of the typical state department of education.
3. What traits would you expect to find in the "intentionally inviting" teacher?
4. Discuss the implications of PL 94-142 and the Americans with Disabilities Act for your anticipated classes.

Chapter 1 Multiple Choice Questions

1. Implicit values of a school are reflected in:
   a. Extrinsic student awards.
   b. Negotiated student-teacher interactions.
   c. The ethos of individual schools.
   d. All of the above.

2. To be "intentionally disinviting" reflects:
   a. Planning, compassion, and understanding.
   b. Teachers who have strong pro-student ideals.
   c. A philosophy of the student as an incompetent person in an impersonal environment.
   d. A teacher who really wants children to learn.

3. Some evidence has been found that teachers treat low achievers in the following manner:
   a. Criticize low achievers often.
   b. Call on low achievers with greater patience.
   c. Provide more wait-time for low achievers.
   d. Seldom criticize low achievers.

4. The actual implementation of an educational goal takes place in:
   a. Society.
   b. A teacher's classroom.
   c. The deliberations of a school board.
   d. The state legislature.

5. The unit of government that has the most control over U.S. public schools:
   a. The state legislature.
   b. Regional cooperative.
   c. The U.S. Department of Education.
   d. The U.S. Supreme Court.

6. One problem identified in the school culture relates to instruction. The authors:
   a. Identify ephemeral norms.
   b. Stress the use of locally prepared instructional materials.
   c. Conclude that instructional methodologies have had a weak research basis.
   d. Provide evidence that state legislatures have remedied instructional problems.

7. "Forget that university nonsense. You're in the real world now" implies that:
   a. You can learn only on the job.
   b. Teaching is not a rational area.
   c. A few people really know what is best.
   d. All of the above.

8. The key incentive for teachers is:
   a. Salary.
   b. The uncertainties of teaching.
   c. Student achievement.
   d. Working alone in the job without interference from others.

9. Which characteristic is essential to be able to do the tough job of teaching?
   a. Conformity to the school's culture.
   b. Using a subject-centered approach.
   c. Having a rationale.
   d. Being efficacious.

10. In general, the school culture is:
    a. Legislated state by state.
    b. Very similar nationally.
    c. Dependent on local norms and values.
    d. Almost identical to that found in the business sector.

11. As a group, new teachers tend to:
    a. Act as change agents in a school.
    b. Resist a subject-centered approach to teaching.
    c. Feel very secure.
    d. Conform to the image of teachers as an authority.
12. Middle school/junior high teachers should particularly consider:
    a. The range of students' cognitive levels.
    b. The need for lectures that stress academic excellence.
    c. The use of lectures as a learning aid.
    d. The implementation of corporal punishment.
13. The basic idea proposed by James Conant in his famous report was that the American comprehensive high school:
    a. Was in need of total revision.
    b. Should be replaced by an entirely new institution.
    c. Simply needed "tuning up."
    d. Should be redesigned to look like its Russian counterpart.
14. The Individual Educational Plan (IEP) requires at least eight elements. Of the four below, which one is NOT required?
    a. Documentation of educational performance.
    b. Identification of family socioeconomic status.
    c. Specification of special services to be delivered.
    d. Evaluation methodology.
15. There is some evidence that the public:
    a. In general is supportive of the schools.
    b. Is very disturbed with the quality of schools.
    c. Believes there is too much emphasis on computers.
    d. Tends to rate their local teachers as impeding school improvement.
16. The concept of the least restrictive environment means:
    a. Every child with any disability must be mainstreamed.
    b. Children with disabilities are separated from regular classes.
    c. Children with disabilities must be treated in a manner similar to children without disabilities.
    d. Children without disabilities have the option to be placed in classes with or without other children having disabilities.

Answer Sheet and Feedback

The responses to the essay questions are simply indicated by showing the pages on which they are addressed in the textbook. The number in parentheses after the correct answer in multiple choice items indicates the page on which the response is located.

Essay Questions

1. Pages 15–16
2. Pages 6–9
3. Page 15
4. Pages 25–28

Multiple Choice Questions

1. d (11–14)
2. c (15)
3. a (17)
4. b (4–5)
5. a (6–7)
6. c (11)
7. d (10–13)
8. c (15–16)
9. d (16)
10. c (3–6, 10–13)
11. d (17–18)
12. a (22–23)
13. c (20)
14. b (25–27)
15. a (30–31)
16. c (26)

Overhead Transparency List

1–1 Advance Organizer
1–2 Contexts of Schooling
1–3 Schools as Governmental Agencies
1–4 School Cultures
1–5 Students
1–6 Diversity Considerations
1–7 Technology

2. The Teacher as Decision Maker

Overview

Chapter 2 orients the reader to selected aspects of the teacher's world of work. We have found that most preservice (and many in-service) teachers do not seriously analyze how and why they teach as they do. By providing a brief introduction about decision making (and then referring back to Chapter 1 where we cover the school cultures, and pluralistic conflicts), your students become more aware that there really is *no* "one best way." Small-group discussions on how to develop a teaching framework will help students to think through the process. The concepts of content and processes of teaching, along with motivation, may need added explanation.

We present the three perspectives of learning and teaching (Developmental, Behavioral, and Constructivist) as these seem to encompass the spectrum for the schools. If your institution has a curriculum laboratory, it would be helpful to assign your students an activity in the lab to compare how a selected program might be taught within these models.

The final part of the chapter attempts to provide a "snapshot" of how school takes place and how there are some well-established traits for effective schools. The points made in Chapter 2 will help counter some of the unwarranted negative press that schooling tends to receive in the media. All these concepts tend to lend themselves to class discussions.

Relevant Student Activities

1. The class might be subdivided into small research groups to determine what decisions are made for the teacher by way of school policy or regulation. This would require an examination of several school policy handbooks. In some states, the state legislature prescribes what can be done in a classroom. These laws might be discussed.
2. Position papers might be assigned to students to examine and compare and contrast the similarities and differences between the three learning and teaching perspectives presented, i.e., Developmental, Behavioral, and Constructivist.
3. Table 3-2, page 56, from John I. Goodlad's popular *A Place Called School* should be discussed in both large and small groups in class. To what extent does it reflect your students' lives in K–12 classes?
4. The eleven effective school correlates might form the basis of a series of student research papers in which individual or small groups could report on current findings.

Topics for Class Discussion

1. How does a teacher education program attempt to develop teaching artistry?
2. Discuss the "If-Then" model of teaching as described on pages 39–40 in the text.
3. What are the instructional implications of adapting some student-initiated learning in a classroom?
4. What does "using developmentally appropriate materials in your classes" really mean? Adversaries might ask, "Is this not just a way of reducing standards even further"?

Focus Resources

We suggest that the following paper be required reading, since it presents insights that do not appear in the popular media.

> Bracey, G. W. "A Nation of Learners: Nostalgia and Amnesia." *Educational Leadership 54*(5) (1997): 53–57.

The class might also examine the Internet site developed by the U.S. Department of Education on cognitive skills.

> Gopher://gopher.ed.gov:70/00/programs/NDN/edprog94/eptw10

Student Evaluation Techniques

The content in Chapter 2 does not lend itself to qualitative methods such as Simulated Classroom Lessons or performance rubrics. We suggest using essay and multiple choice questions.

Suggested Essay Questions

1. How do content and process decisions create problems for teachers?
2. What are at least three basic differences in learning and teaching between the Behavioral and Constructivist perspectives?
3. Discuss four elements of "Effective Schools."
4. Construct a short summary of classroom instruction as presented in the textbook.

Chapter 2 Multiple Choice Questions

1. When a teacher teaches "intuitively," developing lessons on the basis of a feeling for the class, this teacher is using the:
   a. Artistic approach.
   b. Rational planning.
   c. Essentialist-based curriculum.
   d. None of the above.
2. The "If-Then" model to instruction represents an irrational approach to the teaching process.a. True.
   b. False.
3. Research-based teaching is interesting, but of little practical value.
   a. True.
   b. False.
4. Effective schools demonstrate high expectations but do not test to determine student achievement.
   a. True.
   b. False.

5. The text states that the most-used teacher activity at the senior high school level is:
   a. Work on problem solving.
   b. Complex learning skills.
   c. Lecture and recitations.
   d. Student-initiated projects.
6. There is some evidence that over several years:
   a. Classroom instruction has remained rather stable.
   b. Most teachers have become more sensitive to the needs of their learners.
   c. The modern high school stresses life adjustment.
   d. High school teachers use more instructional strategies than any other group of teachers.
7. The importance of the effective-schools research is that it demonstrates:
   a. One best system of instruction exists.
   b. Culture and ethos are combined.
   c. That educationally speaking, "the best will survive."
   d. Schools are effective when certain elements exist.
8. The concrete operational stage is typically characterized by students who:
   a. Learn easily by reading.
   b. Tend to think at formal levels.
   c. Learn concepts by using activities.
   d. Are class discipline problems.
9. A major strength of "Direct Instruction" is that:
   a. Students are free to work on their own.
   b. Content is delivered to all the class simultaneously.
   c. Teacher class preparation is increased dramatically.
   d. Class projects take most of the school time.
10. In Vygotsky's theory, the "zone of proximal development":
    a. Can be enhanced by adult or peer help.
    b. Is fixed for each child.
    c. Is unrelated to child development.
    d. Is a maturational level, similar to Piaget's.
11. Computer-aided instruction is an excellent example of applying which learning theory?
    a. Developmental.
    b. Behavioral.
    c. Constructivist.
    d. Modern social constructivism.
12. Which of the following teacher behaviors is the best example of using student-initiated instruction?
    a. Giving students immediate feedback.
    b. Using variable assignments.
    c. Keeping the class on a time schedule.
    d. Emphasizing basic fundamentals.

13. Active learning:
    a. Applies only to the constructivist philosophy.
    b. Is the hallmark of Vygotsky's ideas.
    c. Implies that there is no feedback to the learner.
    d. Can be used with any learning perspective.

14. Which generalization is most correct or empirically validated?
    a. There is a tendency for elementary teachers to use a wide variety of instructional techniques.
    b. Middle or junior high school teachers have demonstrated the widest array of instructional techniques.
    c. High school teachers have been consistently shown over time to use the widest array of teaching methods.
    d. Teachers at all levels use a very wide array of instructional techniques.

Answer Sheet and Feedback

Essay Questions

1. Pages 39–44
2. Pages 45–54
3. Pages 58–62
4. Pages 54–56

Multiple Choice Questions

1. d (37–38)
2. b (40–41)
3. b (47–49)
4. b (58)
5. c (55–56)
6. a (55)
7. d (54–62)
8. c (45)
9. b (49)
10. a (46)
11. b (49)
12. b (52)
13. d (54)
14. a (56)

Overhead Transparency List

2–1 Advance Organizer
2–2 Teacher as Decision Maker
2–3 Major Teaching and Learning Perspectives
2–4 Characteristics of Effective Schools (a)
2–5 Characteristics of Effective Schools (b)

3. Goals and Outcomes for Instruction

Overview

Chapter 3 initiates the foundational planning process that spans through Chapter 5. Part 1 discusses the roles and potential impact that goals, national and state standards, and local curriculum guidelines play on instructional decision making.

Part 2 emphasizes the manner in which the affective, psychomotor, and cognitive taxonomies aid in planning. We deliberately emphasize the cognitive taxonomy for planning because the major trend is to stress cognitive goals. Our interactive analogue for Bloom's taxonomy is a novel attempt to illustrate how dynamic the levels may well be.

Part 3 stresses the specification of objectives. Again, we stress the performance objective over other models because there is a trend for demonstrated performances to be valued as outcomes of schooling. We close with a short introduction to curriculum alignment as a planning tool.

Relevant Student Activities

1. In a workshop format, assemble sets of the various standards identified on pages 75–76 and 97 in the textbook. Ask the students to identify the kinds of goals and objectives being stressed. Wall charts might be prepared on newsprint and posted for a global view of what content and levels of instruction are warranted.
2. Divide the class into research teams to examine textbooks used in K–12 classes to determine how closely the content parallels that suggested in a relevant national or state standard or guideline.
3. Divide the class into research teams to analyze the questions asked in K–12 textbooks by applying the six levels of the cognitive taxonomy. Graphic displays could be prepared on newsprint to illustrate findings.

Topics for Class Discussion

1. To what extent have the goals of education changed from the classic Seven Cardinal Principles to Goals 2000?
2. How would you (the student) use any of the national standards in modifying your respective classes?
3. To what extent is there any relationship between the affective and cognitive domains?
4. How can the cognitive taxonomic levels aid in planning more effective instruction?
5. To what extent do state curriculum guidelines model instructional alignment?

Focus Resources

In our opinion, there is one paper that thoughtfully presents a strong case for teaching to comprehension. We suggest that it be placed on reserve as required reading.

R. Nickerson. "Understanding Understanding." *American Journal of Education 93* (1985): 201–239.

Class members might be encouraged to seek updated information about Goals 2000 and congressional and U.S. Department of Education position papers on that Web site.

http://www.ed.gov/legislation/GOALS2000/index.html

Student Evaluation Techniques

Qualitative Method

Students could be assigned the task of preparing a series of learner outcomes or objectives that span the six levels of the cognitive taxonomy. These could be assigned from the content in Chapter 3 of the textbook or from a K–12 textbook in their respective areas of specialization. A scoring rubric could be constructed to show how this task would be evaluated.

Suggested Essay Questions

1. Compare the structure of the affective domain with that of the cognitive domain.
2. Provide two models of goals statements and show they are either different or similar to objectives.
3. Other than Goals 2000, who are the primary writers of national standards?
4. How is mastery learning different from outcomes-based education? How is it similar?

Chapter 3 Multiple Choice Questions

1. The statement "to prepare the best teachers in the state" would be classified as (a/an)
   a. Criterion measure.
   b. Goal.
   c. Specified outcome.
   d. Performance objective.
2. An apparent underlying motive for Goals 2000 is:
   a. To create a more educationally sensitive society.
   b. Educational excellence.
   c. Globally economic challenges.
   d. The desire for social justice.
3. To date, a sampling of major school reform movements as illustrated in various reports shows:
   a. There is a designed vision of improvement.
   b. There is dramatic improvement in achievement.
   c. Needed changes are now implemented.
   d. There are many changes, but few that are substantive.
4. Performance objectives help to clarify instruction for:
   a. Students as they study.
   b. Teachers as they plan for instruction.
   c. Items a and b are both correct.
   d. None of the above is correct.

5. Which is the most accurate assessment of the performance objective movement?
   a. The emphasis is on student outputs.
   b. The emphasis is on what the teacher does (inputs).
   c. There is no evidence to show that performance objectives work in classrooms.
   d. It is an "anti-accountability" technique.

6. A teacher who uses performance objectives correctly will:
   a. Assign only A and B grades.
   b. Use only satisfactory and unsatisfactory in grading.
   c. Establish grading criteria.
   d. Will not assign grades at all.

7. The authors would view performance objectives as:
   a. An absolute educational necessity.
   b. One technique by which to specify instruction.
   c. The only technique that a teacher may use.
   d. Quite really, a big waste of teacher's time.

8. Which item is NOT a part of a performance objective?
   a. Criterion.
   b. Performance.
   c. Condition.
   d. Rationale.

9. Curriculum alignment refers to:
   a. Assessment, instruction, and observations.
   b. Goals, the society, and the culture.
   c. Assessment, values, and observations.
   d. Learning objectives, assignments, instruction, and tests.

10. To align the curriculum in part means to:
   a. File performance objectives.
   b. Explicitly test what is explicitly taught.
   c. Compare standardized test results with other schools nationally.
   d. Test students on every possible learning objective.

Below are three paired statements, e.g., 11a and 11b. For each pair, mark your answer for the objective that best meets the requirements for a performance objective.

11. a. Develop one roll of black and white film.
    b. Understand how a developing agent works.

12. a. Select six useful objectives.
    b. Know what makes six objectives useful.

13. a. Select from alternatives those definitions which best define the terms.
    b. Appreciate all the meanings of the terms.

Categorize the objectives or assignments illustrated in items 14–16 as to their taxonomic level.

14. After reading the two short stories, write a three-page paper comparing the idea of "hero" as viewed in both stories.
   a. Knowledge.
   b. Application.
   c. Analysis.
   d. Evaluation.

15. Given a newspaper article from a newspaper, the student will summarize the article and include at least three major points.
    a. Knowledge.
    b. Comprehension.
    c. Analysis.
    d. Evaluation.

16. Develop a plan that tests the efficacy of two different fertilizers in growing flowers.
    a. Comprehension.
    b. Application.
    c. Analysis.
    d. Synthesis.

Answer Sheet and Feedback

Essay Questions

1. Pages 78 and 94
2. Pages 69–71, 98–100
3. Pages 74–75
4. Pages 96–103

Multiple Choice Questions

1. b (69–70)
2. c (72–74)
3. d (74–75)
4. c (98–99, 103)
5. a (98)
6. c (101–103)
7. b (103)
8. d (98)
9. d (104–105)
10. b (104)
11. a (98–100)
12. a (98–100)
13. a (98–100)
14. c (84–85)
15. b (80–82)
16. d (85–87)

Overhead Transparency List

3–1 Advance Organizer
3–2 Goals and Standards
3–3 Domains of Learning
3–4 Cognitive Taxonomy
3–5 Cognitive Taxonomy Models
3–6 Interactive Cognitive Taxonomy
3–7 Taxonomy Uses
3–8 A Model of Teaching Alignment

4. INSTRUCTIONAL DESIGN

Overview

Lesson designing and planning are two activities where teachers in the field spend a few seconds per day to sketch an outline or hours to design elaborate models. Our goal is to illustrate a variety of ideas using Louis Sullivan's dictum that "form follows function." We stress daily planning, unit planning, and long-range planning. We also suggest reviewing Chapter 3, where the topics of goals and outcomes are introduced as well as Chapter 1, where we introduced IEP.

We recognize that fads abound in the educational enterprise with some lesson plan designers having vastly oversold their ideas, and we do caution the instructor in that regard.

Part 1 of the chapter stresses the importance of preparing for lesson planning, including the use of publishers' teacher aids. Part 2 illustrates ideals that can provide for different ways of organizing lessons—thematic units, units. We reinforce the notions of goals and outcomes that are presented in Chapter 3. The Kaplan Matrix on page 129 will be a very handy planning tool. An actual lesson plan is illustrated on pages 132 and 133 in the text.

Part 3 is an empirically derived illustration of how expert teachers plan. The concepts of routines, reflection, independent planning levels, and the treasury of teaching materials may be a surprise to many preservice students—and to practicing teachers.

Relevant Student Activities

1. Give each student a blank lesson plan format. Have students each complete a lesson plan for the next class session. The lesson plans should incorporate all parts of the lesson plan as discussed in Chapter 4 of *Teaching Strategies.*

2. During the next class session, divide the class into their respective content areas. Have each group critique each other's individual lesson plans, making sure all parts are included. As a group, work together to complete each lesson plan as needed. Note: This activity could also be used as a qualitative evaluation technique.

3. After examining the Kaplan Matrix in Tables 4.1 and 4.2 in *Teaching Strategies,* divide the class into groups of four. Distribute a blank Kaplan Matrix to each group.

4. Interview a teacher in a public school. What routines, sources of information, and thoughts guide this teacher as a unit or daily lesson is planned?

5. Obtain information from a school district illustrating the types of lesson plans the district requires the teachers to file. Evaluate those requirements in light of the lesson plan elements discussed in *Teaching Strategies.*

Topics for Class Discussion

1. List and describe each part of the lesson plan as described in *Teaching Strategies.* What benefit does each part of the lesson plan provide in the overall plan?

2. Critique each of the lesson plan formats provided. Which one appeals to you? Why?

3. How could Lazear's multiple intelligences toolbox, shown in Table 4.3, be used as a lesson planning device?

Focus Resources

We strongly recommend placing on reserve a research review illustrating differences between how teachers are taught to plan instruction and how at least some teachers actually do such planning. This classic article could serve as a discussion topic for "theoretical versus practical" in instructional planning.

Brown, D. S. "Twelve Middle-School Teachers' Planning." *The Elementary School Journal* 89(1) (1988): 69–87.

Rather than providing one Internet site for examination, we present a very useful paper that describes a plethora of Web sites relating to social studies. You'll find lesson plans, resources, and documents to make social studies more exciting. A wide range of governmental, organizational, and individual sites are listed.

Levine, M. G. "Social Studies Web Sites for Teachers and Students." *Social Studies Review 36*(2) (1997): 95–98.

Student Evaluation Techniques

Qualitative Method

1. Establish a grading rubric for construction of a unit plan. Assign either individuals or small groups the task of crafting a unit plan for some prescribed period of time.

Suggested Essay Questions

1. How have teachers applied "reflective practices" in their lesson planning?
2. Illustrate how knowledge, skill, and attitudinal outcomes differ instructionally.
3. How could you use two of the seven multiple intelligences in designing a content-concept lesson?
4. What differentiates a lesson plan from an activity plan?

Chapter 4 Multiple Choice Questions

1. In lesson planning, the term "unit" best describes:
   a. An outline of how the lesson will be taught.
   b. The name of the larger element of instruction of which the particular lesson is part.
   c. A brief justification of why students should learn what is being taught.
   d. A checklist of everything the student needs.
2. In lesson planning, the term "instructional goal" best describes:
   a. A detailed outline of what is to be taught.
   b. A brief description of what the students will do as a consequence of the lesson.
   c. An outline of student entry-level behaviors.
   d. Post-instruction assessment of student performance.

3. In lesson planning, the term *rationale* best describes:
   a. A brief justification of why students should learn what is being taught.
   b. A description of what students will be able to do as a consequence of the lesson.
   c. An outline of how the lesson will be taught.
   d. Outcomes students are to achieve on completion of the total unit of instruction.
4. Prelesson preparation includes preparation and assessment of:
   a. Lesson evaluation and revision notes.
   b. Goals, objectives, rationale, and content.
   c. Goals, content, student entry level, and student activities.
   d. Rationale, content, procedures, and evaluation.
5. Which is the best example of a student learning goal? The students will:
   a. List five of the original thirteen colonies.
   b. Present a three-minute oral report about a current issue.
   c. Communicate effectively in a variety of ways.
   d. Analyze a written report for clarity and cohesiveness.
6. Lesson plans have value in that they:
   a. Keep the principal off "your case."
   b. Articulate the teacher's ideas, activities, and assignments.
   c. Assist only beginning teachers.
   d. Can be used year after year without modification.
7. The best technique for obtaining information regarding student background or entry level would be:
   a. Observation in hallways.
   b. Sociodemographic analysis.
   c. Personal opinion.
   d. Review of the cumulative folder.
8. Specific learning outcomes specify:
   a. Student concepts to be learned.
   b. Student observable behaviors.
   c. Student achievement data.
   d. Student attitudes.
9. The authors strongly suggest that:
   a. Lesson plans be evaluated after use.
   b. Lesson design is truly an "art."
   c. Teachers do not reflect on lesson design.
   d. The school districts require new plans each year
10. One aspect of planning in which expert teachers differ from novice teachers is in:
   a. Using a limited set of resources.
   b. Using interdependent planning levels.
   c. Establishing necessary content and procedures.
   d. Specifying goals and outcomes.
11. Assessment of student achievement is done to:
   a. Satisfy state laws.
   b. Give evidence of work done by individuals.
   c. Assess school-wide achievement.
   d. Avoid giving frequent tests.

12. Effective teachers use old lesson plans to begin new plans.
    a. True
    b. False
13. Objectives in a Kaplan Matrix are organized and presented in an hierarchical fashion.
    a. True
    b. False
14. Specifying a rationale clarifies the lesson intent.
    a. True
    b. False

Answer Sheet and Feedback

Essay Questions

1. Page 135
2. Pages 124–129
3. Pages 129–130
4. Pages 130–132

Multiple Choice Questions

1. b. (119–120)
2. b (112–113)
3. a (122–123)
4. c (117–119)
5. c (123–125)
6. b (112–113)
7. d (118)
8. b (118)
9. a (134)
10. b (135–136)
11. b (130)
12. a (136)
13. a (128–129)
14. a (122–123)

Overhead Transparency List

4–1 Advance Organizer
4–2 Prelesson Considerations
4–3 Lesson Planning Information Sources
4–4 Lesson Planning Cycle
4–5 Unit Planning
4–6 Lesson Planning Suggestions
4–7 Expert Teachers' Planning

5. Sequencing Instruction

Overview

Chapter 5 contains four interrelated parts, all with the purpose of showing how to make complex concepts more teachable and, of greater importance, more learnable. Part 1 presents some introductory aspects of sequencing and basic content forms, closing with a lucid model of inductive and deductive modes of presentation.

Part 2 illustrates three models for organizing lessons or units of instruction. Beginning teachers tend not to organize concepts, generalizations, or principles that are embodied in a discipline or subject area into an integrated whole, nor do they usually subdivide difficult topics. There are several approaches that have been successfully used to accomplish that planning. The models are only illustrative of an array of those available to teachers. The Concept Analysis Model is primarily cognitive. The Task Analysis Model tends to be linear and sequential whereas the Advance Organizer Model, if all components are used, is very interactive as is the Concept Analysis Model. Common features of all the models stress that meaningful learning is subdivided into parts. In that manner, the intended information can be understood and is sequenced so that the parts contribute to understanding a body of knowledge. Each of the models aids understanding in a different way. Teachers make decisions as to which model is most appropriate for the content being learned. It is suggested that students have an experience with each of the models in this chapter. It is important to analyze each experience so that students understand the common lesson planning principles embedded in each model. Further, students must understand the unique features of each model.

Parts 3 and 4 tend to merge the notion of how humans learn. Part 3 introduces the exciting concepts of brain hemisphericity, while Part 4 briefly examines the popular idea of learning styles. We recommend revisiting pages 129 and 130 in Chapter 4 to expand Table 4.3 of David Lazear's "Multiple Intelligences Toolbox."

Relevant Student Activities

1. For a task analysis activity, divide the class in subject area groups. Each group will decide on a single, but rather difficult, lesson performance objective. Have each group prepare a task analysis of the objective, recording the results on newsprint or an overhead transparency. Have the group present their work to the class. After several presentations, discuss advantages and problems of task analysis.

2. Have each student develop a lesson plan and demonstrate the Concept Analysis Model with the Advance Organizer Model. Depending on the size of the class, you can either have each student micro-teach or divide the class so that one-half presents the Concept Analysis Model and one-half the Advance Organizer Model. Discuss content appropriate for each model.

3. A brainstormed chart describing the common and unique lesson planning characteristics of each model provides an excellent chapter summary activity.

4. Assign the topics of hemisphericity, learning styles, and multiple intelligences as the focus for small-group research reports. Emphasize the location of published papers in *refereed research journals.* Any surprises?

5. If you should have a practicum or observation component associated with the course, then ask students to use one of the models or have them identify lessons from which one of the models is appropriate and actually conduct a lesson.

Topics for Class Discussion

1. Describe how you could use task analysis in lesson planning.
2. What are similarities and differences between task analysis and concept analysis?
3. What value do hierarchies and sequencing have for student learning?
4. How could a classroom teacher accommodate the learning styles of every student being taught? (Hint: 28 students in K–6 classes, 100 per teacher in middle schools, and about 150 in high schools.)
5. What advantages or disadvantages does the concept of multiple intelligences have over learning styles?

Focus Resources

The following book is a volume illustrating a rich series of graphic, visual, and task organizers. Students will benefit greatly by perusing it.

Tarquin, P. and S. Walker. *Creating Success in the Classroom: Visual Organizers and How to Use Them.* Englewood, CO: Teachers Ideas Press, 1997, 235 pp.

You and your students will find the Web site below an expansion of ideas and inventories relating to *learning styles.*

http://www.oise.utoronto.ca/~ggay/lstests.htm

Student Evaluation Techniques

Suggested Essay Questions

1. Select a concept from your area of specialization and create a learning hierarchy chart illustrating the dependent and independent sequences needed for student success.
2. Illustrate two different ways that you could use an advance organizer to initiate a lesson.
3. How do learning modalities differ from multiple intelligences?
4. Select some concept from your specialization. Focus student activities to accommodate left and right hemispheric functions.

Chapter 5 Multiple Choice Questions

1. Task analysis reflects which assumption?
   a. Communicating to students what is to be taught is confusing to them.
   b. Learning is somewhat random in the schools, thus, it helps to add a sequence.
   c. The schools must help students to appreciate our culture in the best possible manner.
   d. Teaching tasks sequentially has been and continues to be critical in creating student success.

2. An example of teaching at the concrete level of a concept hierarchy is:
   a. Discussing nutrient needs in the human body.
   b. Predicting the changing dietary needs of humans.
   c. Introducing the Food Guide Pyramid on an overhead as a dietary guide.
   d. Identifying links between specific dietary deficiencies and health problems.

3. Which statement is most valid?
   a. Dependent sequences are less crucial than independent sequences when diagnosing learner difficulties.
   b. It is not possible to sequence material dependently to make a learning prescription.
   c. When student difficulty is diagnosed, dependent sequencing is especially useful in developing a prescription to improve learning.
   d. When student difficulty is diagnosed, sequencing is then done by the students.

4. Which set of action verbs would imply the simplest set of learning objectives if you were using task analysis?
   a. Interpret, illustrate, judge, solve.
   b. Define, record, cite, identify.
   c. List, compile, solve, explain.
   d. Estimate, contrast, judge, rate.

5. Advance organizers provide for:
   a. Six-step interaction models.
   b. "Ideational scaffolds."
   c. Concept sequencing.
   d. Terminal objectives.

6. Ausubel's Model is most nearly an example of:
   a. Deductive presentations.
   b. Mastery learning.
   c. Inductive presentations.
   d. Hypothetico-deductive presentations.

7. From the following choices, select the beginning phase of Ausubel's Model.
   a. In-depth studies of a variety of issues which affect families.
   b. A presentation of the family within society and identification of issues affecting families.
   c. A discussion predicting how changes in society will affect families.
   d. A survey of the class understanding of the issues which affect families.

8. Which student activities would be oriented toward the brain's right hemisphere:
   a. What meaning is derived from this cartoon about the president?
   b. What does the table on page 182 show?
   c. How many specific traits of the president does the cartoon illustrate?
   d. What conclusions can be reached from the data on page 182?

9. You have a student who you diagnose as being "field-dependent." Which traits below led you to that conclusion?
   a. Loves to work independently.
   b. Favorite subject is computer programming.
   c. Works crossword puzzles in spare time.
   d. Tells you how enjoyable committee work is.

10. One student seems to show a preference for stories that are filled with human interactions, and also narrates very colorful stories. You think you might have a student who fits Gregorc's category of being:
    a. Abstract sequential.
    b. Emotional abstract.
    c. Abstract random.
    d. Abstract dependent.
11. One learning-style advocate who attempts to incorporate experiences and thinking somewhat similar to Bloom's Taxonomy is:
    a. R. Dunn.
    b. A. Gregorc.
    c. H. Gardner.
    d. B. McCarthy.
12. Which conclusion would be the most accurate regarding learning styles?
    a. Incorporating learning styles in a classroom probably won't hurt anyone.
    b. Large-scale major research projects strongly validate learning styles.
    c. Researchers have evidence that incorporating learning styles is a very simple classroom procedure.
    d. Learning modalities have been very thoroughly negated by research done in New Zealand.
13. In practice, when you use a task analysis, you define separate tasks before ordering them.
    a. True
    b. False
14. In general, it makes little difference how or when a teacher introduces items arranged in a dependent sequence.
    a. True
    b. False
15. Using a hierarchy chart, such as Gagne's, requires the students to sequence the way they complete the assignment.
    a. True
    b. False

Answer Sheet and Feedback

Essay Questions

1. Pages 148–151, 156–157
2. Pages 159–163
3. Pages 172–174
4. Pages 164–166

Multiple Choice Questions

1. d (148)
2. c (150–152)
3. c (154)
4. b (148–149)
5. b (159–160)
6. a (159)
7. b (159–161)
8. a (164–165)
9. d (167)
10. c (169–170)
11. d (171–172)
12. a (172–173)
13. a (153–156)
14. b (154, 158)
15. b (148–150)

Overhead Transparency List

5–1 Advance Organizer
5–2 Sequencing
5–3 Hierarchy
5–4 Content Forms
5–5 Presentation Modes
5–6 Models of Lesson Organization
5–7 Task Analysis
5–8 Concept Analysis
5–9 Advance Organizer
5–10 Hemisphericity
5–11 Learning Styles
5–12 Learning Differences
5–13 Learning Styles Approaches
5–14 Multiple Intelligences

6. Managing the Classroom Environment

Overview

Chapter 6 provides an introduction to classroom management concepts and strategies. Our goal is that prospective teachers leave this chapter with an understanding of the many management variables that exist in the classroom. We also hope every novice teacher begins to develop a philosophy for approaching management issues. Within this context, classroom management strategies and accompanying research are presented in a fashion that enables new teachers to understand the principles and the underlying support in the literature for the strategy presented.

We stress the negative impact on learning of laissez-faire classroom management practices and stress the need for teachers to thoroughly investigate management techniques and evolve a set of classroom practice and theories that will maximize a successful learning environment.

Parts 1 and 2 suggest positive classroom environments based on adherence to norms and awareness of the classroom environment. These are supported by six elements of effective teaching by planning for classroom routines, establishing only usable rules, getting off to a good start, monitoring the class continuously, keeping records efficiently, and creating strategies for managing interruptions.

Part 3 illustrates a continuum of management systems. Self-discipline systems, which include the hierarchy of needs, moral reasoning, and teacher effectiveness training, also stress personal responsibilities. Imposed-discipline systems, such as desist strategies and behavior modification, stress teacher authority, while behavioral systems require pinpointing of specific behaviors and using reinforcers.

In Part 4, we note four major points: (1) positive environment stresses equity as a major principle; (2) homogeneous grouping may not be instructionally effective; (3) parental involvement aids in achieving school expectations, so teachers should build positive relationships with parents; and (4) teachers must learn to recognize the signs of child abuse and drug and alcohol abuse so that they can work with the proper authorities.

Relevant Student Activities

It is important that prospective teachers have the opportunity of observing and testing the various classroom strategies identified here. We suggest implementing a three-phase technique with observation, testing and commitment.

1. Place students in a variety of classrooms that stress differing approaches to classroom management. Request that the students chart the various teacher-student interactions and note the amount of student time spent on nonlearning activities. Discuss the impact of various classroom management strategies and the impact on "time-on-learning."

2. Provide the students with opportunities to practice various strategies. Such testing can occur in a regular classroom or through videotaped SCL. Pair your students to allow charting and measurement of effectiveness.

3. Group students by classroom management interest. Have the student groups create a supportive environment and further their personal interest through research, demonstrations, observations, and feedback during teaching episodes.

Topics for Class Discussion

1. To what extent would you argue that classroom management is just discipline? What are the implications of this assertion for a teacher's choice of management systems?
2. How would you create a classroom management system if you have not experienced one in operation?
3. In what ways might increased family mobility require teachers to take a different approach to classroom management than previously used?
4. How might classroom norms, power relationships, and teacher awareness affect a teacher's implementation of a planned lesson?
5. What should you consider when preparing a lesson plan that anticipates interruptions?
6. Reality therapy stresses teacher involvement. To what extent is it reasonable or unreasonable to expect a teacher to become involved with the problems of every student?
7. Why are verbal and nonverbal behaviors important teachers' tools for classroom interaction and reinforcement?

Focus Resources

The following paper illustrates ways of determining a classroom's environment to enhance student performance.

Stewart, S. C., W. H. Evans and D. J. Kacznski. "Setting the Stage for Success: Assessing the Instructional Environment." *Preventing School Failure 41*(2) (1997): 53–56.

The Web site below explores the concepts proposed by Randall Sprick, a widely cited classroom management specialist. Explore it for useful ideas.

http://www.state.ky.us/agencies/behave/chaos1.html

Student Evaluation Techniques

Qualitative Method

On the first day of class, hand out three 3x5 cards to each student and ask your students to briefly describe a classroom management/student behavior problem on each card.

Measurement Strategy A—From time to time during the course, have a student randomly select a card and provide a classroom management solution compatible with recent instruction.

Measurement Strategy B—Select a study group to identify a compatible management solution plan and then demonstrate the solution while being videotaped.

Suggested Essay Questions

Below is a series of five "mini" cases. In each case, the teacher, Pat Taylor, takes some action. You must determine what management strategy was employed. On your answer sheet, identify each management strategy employed that needs to be determined as either Behavior Modification, Desist Strategy, Reality Therapy, or Self-Discipline. Following your answer, please briefly explain your choice.

1. Pat has had much trouble with Randy E. No homework has been handed in for six to seven assignments. Pat discusses Randy's problem with him. Randy writes out a plan to finish his assignments. What strategy is being employed?
2. Michael S. was whispering "sweet nothings" to his classmate across the row. Pat notices this and gives both Michael and friend a chilling glance. What strategy is being used?
3. Pat was transferred to the junior high to help out with a "tough" class. A meeting was held between Pat and the two counselors and the principal. This group planned a technique that would be applied for effective management. All agreed that Pat would have to use reinforcers, such as snacks, school supplies, and free time to change student behaviors. What strategy is being used?
4. The principal of Pat's school met with all the teachers to decide on a uniform discipline plan based on set consequences that all teachers could use. What strategy is being used?
5. Pat's principal asks her to actively involve her students in assessing and modifying their own behaviors. What strategy does the principal want Pat to use?

Chapter 6 Multiple Choice Questions

1. Which of the following is NOT an acceptable classroom management strategy for changing unacceptable behaviors.
   a. Offer rewards for appropriate behaviors.
   b. Lower grades for inappropriate behaviors.
   c. Set consequences for inappropriate behaviors.
   d. State rules up-front without waiting to see how your students behave.
2. In Maslow's hierarchy of needs, discipline is based on:
   a. Moving students up the hierarchy as fast as possible.
   b. Meeting self-actualization needs before physiological needs.
   c. Addressing student needs to eliminate the behavior problem.
   d. Stabilizing students at one level of the hierarchy.
3. Kohlberg supports the teaching of moral reasoning so that:
   a. Students will have a feeling that there is one right solution to problems.
   b. Students can learn to manage their lives from an ethical perspective.
   c. Students can make quick decisions.
   d. Students can learn to manage their lives by following the set rules of each society.
4. Reality Therapy emphasizes:
   a. Preselection of consequences and punishment.
   b. Teaching students to take responsibility for their own behavior.
   c. Sending students to the principal's office to relieve teachers from undue responsibility.
   d. Discipline based on the teacher's constant monitoring of students.
5. Desist Strategies require the teacher to do three of the following. Which one is NOT a desist strategy?
   a. Allowing students to self-monitor behaviors.
   b. Specifying appropriate behaviors before an activity begins.
   c. Using the lowest level of force possible.
   d. Using private forms of communication whenever possible to reprimand students.

6. A Desist technique using public communication might be needed when:
   a. A student has repeatedly forgotten homework.
   b. A student "doodles" during a recitation period.
   c. A student keeps talking to a peer during quiet time.
   d. Two students are fighting.

7. Self-Discipline emphasizes:
   a. Student autonomy in solving behavior problems.
   b. Tolerance of individual behaviors and needs.
   c. Ordained, uniform rewards and punishments for behaviors.
   d. The need for individual teachers to set their own standards.

8. One reason for removing the reinforcer in behavior modification is to:
   a. Punish the child for inappropriate behaviors.
   b. Test the effectiveness of the intervention.
   c. Prevent teacher burn-out on the behavior modification system.
   d. To switch to more negative consequences when behavior remains a problem.

9. In designing discipline plans, it is best to:
   a. Start with expectations for small improvements in behavior.
   b. Start with expectations for big improvements in behavior.
   c. Set final goals and expect students to reach them quickly.
   d. Emphasize punishment over reward when students are difficult.

10. Management problems occur frequently:
    a. When the teacher sets the classroom rules.
    b. During transitions from one activity to another.
    c. When computer instruction is taking place.
    d. During small group discussions.

11. Sudden behavioral changes may indicate:
    a. Use of alcohol or drugs.
    b. Family problems.
    c. Child abuse.
    d. All of the above.

Answer Sheet and Feedback

Essay Questions

1. Reality Therapy (Pages 196–200)
2. Desist Strategies (Pages 200–203)
3. Behavior Modification (Pages 203–208)
4. Self-Discipline (Pages 194–195)
5. Reality Therapy (Pages 196–200)

Multiple Choice Questions

1. b (184–186, 207–208)
2. c (193–194)
3. b (194–195)
4. b (196–197)
5. a (200–201)
6. d (201–202)
7. c (193–195)
8. b (206–207)
9. a (183–185)
10. b (189–191)
11. d (214–216)

Overhead Transparency List

6–1 Advance Organizer
6–2 Goals of Classroom Management
6–3 Classroom Routines
6–4 Anticipated Interruptions
6–5 Unanticipated Interruptions
6–6 Continuum of Classroom Management Systems
6–7 Hierarchy of Needs (Maslow)
6–8 Reality Therapy (Glasser)
6–9 Moral Reasoning (Kohlberg)
6–10 Desist Strategies—Levels of Force
6–11 Desist Strategies—Type
6–12 Behavior Modification
6–13 Effective Classroom Management
6–14 Issues in Management

7. The Process of Questioning

Overview

Chapter 7 illustrates the use of a systematic method of conducting traditional recitation periods. The evidence overwhelmingly favors the "wait time" technique, so that those who want to refute it must provide substantive evidence to the contrary! Our goal is to show how to develop a repertoire of question-asking skills, so that teaching behaviors reflect a consistent and positive approach to verbal interactions.

Collectively, the five parts of the chapter are designed to illustrate: (1) how to use questions effectively, (2) ways of devising questions, (3) appropriate teacher behaviors in conducting recitations, (4) methods of increasing student participation in the recitations, and (5) teacher idiosyncrasies that actually interfere with the smooth flow of classroom verbal interactions.

Our experience has been that this chapter should be followed immediately by a videotaped teaching (SCL) experience so that all students can apply selected techniques. We encourage the course instructor to discuss the concept of "equity of classroom participation" so that prospective or in-service teachers truly realize that all students must be treated equitably during the classroom recitation periods.

Relevant Student Activities

1. Students brainstorm stimulating topics for recitations from their content/teaching areas. Students then practice posing a question to the class and generating an interactive recitation that utilizes good questioning techniques. (Do this prior to Simulated Classroom Lessons.)

2. Before Simulated Classroom Lessons, have students generate a list of questions (using different levels of questioning as in Bloom's taxonomy) that they may use during their SLC. This would be a good place to apply the Kaplan Grid (pages 128–129).

3. Ask the students to tabulate a series of questions asked by their college professors. Tabulations should follow a uniform method or code. From the data, students should be able to conclude whether professors ask questions in any systematic patterns and if there is any gender bias during class periods.

4. Divide students into groups of three and assign each of these topics related to good questioning techniques.

   - Wait Time I, II.
   - Handling incorrect responses.
   - Promoting multiple responses.
   - Encouraging nonvolunteers.
   - Not attending to responding students.
   - Always selecting same respondents.

Have each group develop a skit of a teacher in a classroom to show: (a) what happens in classrooms when these skills are *not* used appropriately, and (b) what happens in classrooms when these skills *are* used in appropriate ways.

Topics for Class Discussion

1. Why is it important to use higher-level questioning?
2. You are a teacher. Choose a grade level to simulate. The students in your class are not comfortable with using higher-level thinking skills. How would you go about teaching them to use higher-level thinking skills?
3. Describe the teacher idiosyncrasies that tend to interfere with verbal interaction in the classroom. What can you do to avoid these?
4. Reflect on your own K–12 schooling experiences. What questioning techniques were used by your "best" and "worst" teachers?
5. How can you best develop "student questions" in your class recitations?

Focus Resources

The following monograph is an excellent source on how to get students to ask questions of their texts. The authors emphasize reading, but remember, reading is universal in schooling, thus the hints have wide applicability. A word of caution: What the authors incorrectly call "discussion" is what we correctly label as "recitation."

> Beck, I. L., M. G. Mckeown, R. L. Hamilton, and L. Kucan. *Questioning the Author: An Approach for Enhancing Student Engagement with Text.* Newark, DE: International Reading Association, 1997, 122 pp.

An interesting Internet site called "Filling the Toolbox" provides added classroom strategies to encourage student questioning. We suggest that it be examined and used as a discussion topic.

> http://www.pacificrim.net/~mckenzie/toolbox.html

Student Evaluation Techniques

Suggested Essay Questions

1. How could you use "concept mapping" to stimulate your students to generate questions?
2. How does the logic of a question affect its response?
3. Questions may be classified as convergent, divergent, and evaluative.
   a. Define each of these types.
   b. Give an example of each (in the form of a question).
   c. How do these relate to Bloom's taxonomy? Knowledge, comprehension, application, analysis, evaluation, synthesis.
4. Below are seven techniques for promoting questioning in the classroom. For each one, describe the technique and then give an example of how you would use each, or write/act out a scenario of a classroom scene and demonstrate how you would use each.
   - Wait Time I, II.
   - Handling incorrect responses.
   - Promoting multiple responses.
   - Encouraging nonvolunteers.

- Allowing students to complete their responses.
- Attending to responding students.
- Selecting different respondents.

Chapter 7 Multiple Choice Questions

1. Teachers in classrooms tend to ask most questions at the following cognitive level:
   a. Knowledge.
   b. Comprehension.
   c. Application.
   d. Evaluation.

2. When teachers systematically raise their level of questioning:
   a. Students get confused and become frustrated.
   b. Students tend to respond with higher level answers.
   c. The quantity of questions becomes more important than the quality.
   d. Questions tend to become haphazard.

3. Questioning is most effective as a teaching tool when:
   a. One questioning strategy is adopted for all teaching situations.
   b. Students are encouraged to ask their own questions.
   c. Questioning is random and sporadic.
   d. Questions are geared to those students with the highest abilities.

4. Questions may be best classified as:
   a. Convergent, inquiry, divergent.
   b. Simple, complex, mediary.
   c. Convergent, divergent, evaluative.
   d. Evaluative, assessment, analysis.

5. Convergent levels of questioning:
   a. Promote higher level thinking, such as analysis and synthesis.
   b. Encourage exploration of topics.
   c. Promote student-directed instruction.
   d. Are lower levels of questioning related to knowledge and comprehension.

6. Divergent levels of questioning encourage:
   a. Multiple student responses.
   b. One "right-answer" responses.
   c. Thinking at lower knowledge and comprehension levels.
   d. Teacher-directed discussions.

7. Which of the following is NOT an appropriate use for questioning?
   a. A teacher uses questioning to discipline a student who has not read the homework assignment.
   b. A teacher uses questioning to find out how much his or her students know about a topic prior to studying the topic.
   c. A teacher asks knowledge and application questions to review for a test in health.
   d. A teacher prompts students when they cannot answer the question.

8. Wait Time I involves these steps:
   a. Ask a question, call on a student, wait a few seconds for a response.
   b. Call on a student, ask a question, wait for a few seconds for a response.
   c. Ask a question, wait a few seconds, call on a student.
   d. Wait 5 seconds between questions for students to make transitions in thinking.

9. Wait Time II requires the teacher to:
   a. Ask a question, call on a student, wait for a full minute for a response.
   b. Pause after a student responds to a question to allow the student more time to think and respond further.
   c. Wait indefinitely for students who seem unsure of themselves to respond.
   d. Give the student hints if they cannot come up with the answer.

10. Wait time has the following effects:
    a. Teachers tend to repeat themselves more.
    b. Teachers ask more lower level questions.
    c. Fewer students answer the questions.
    d. Students give more complex and complete answers.

11. When a student does not correctly answer a question, the teacher should:
    a. Quickly call on another student to avoid embarrassment.
    b. Use positive reinforcement to prompt the student.
    c. Ignore the student's response and go on.
    d. Tell the student what is wrong with the answer.

12. What would be the best teacher response if a student gives an incorrect response?
    a. "That's not right, but don't worry, I'll call on someone else."
    b. "I'm not sure you read the assignment."
    c. "Tell us some more . . . how did you come to that conclusion?"
    d. "Interesting . . . but not what I'm looking for."

13. Multiple responses can be encouraged by:
    a. Asking divergent or evaluative questions.
    b. Asking convergent, specific questions.
    c. Asking one student to correct another's response.
    d. Asking each student different, relevant questions.

14. One way to encourage nonvolunteers to respond during class discussion is to:
    a. Wait until they respond.
    b. Ask them to reveal the assignment.
    c. Prepare the students the day before with the questions you may ask in class.
    d. Take away discussion points for those who do not participate.

15. In conducting class recitations, teachers should:
    a. Concentrate on asking a few highly verbal students to respond.
    b. Complete student responses for the student who has partially completed a response.
    c. Call on only those students who have their hands up.
    d. Make sure all students are given time to respond.

16. Teacher idiosyncrasies that interfere with smooth verbal interaction in the classroom include:
    a. Repeating the students' response.
    b. Repeating the question.
    c. Answering the question.
    d. All of the above.

17. You tabulate the number of teacher questions asked during a 20-minute recitation period and note that 40 questions were asked. From these data, the most valid inference would be that:
    a. The teacher is using wait time properly.
    b. Students are not responding properly.
    c. Questions are being asked of only a few students.
    d. Questions are probably at the knowledge level.

18. Concept review involves the process of:
    a. Going over new material a minimum of three times.
    b. Making up a guide for testing.
    c. Relating previously learned concepts to new concepts you are teaching.
    d. Repeating information and concepts learned the week before.

Answer Sheet and Feedback

Essay Questions

1. Pages 233–234
2. Pages 224–226
3. Pages 228–233
4. Pages 234–248

Multiple Choice Questions

1. a (221–223)
2. b (223–225)
3. b (224–225)
4. c (227)
5. d (228)
6. a (229–231)
7. a (235–236)
8. c (235–236)
9. b (235–237)
10. d (237)
11. b (237–241)
12. c (239–240)
13. a (229–231)
14. c (245–246)
15. d (250)
16. d (248–250)
17. d (221–223)
18. c (243–244)

Overhead Transparency List

7–1 Advance Organizer
7–2 Questioning Overview
7–3 Basic Questioning Categories
7–4 Concept Mapping
7–5 Questioning Considerations
7–6 Wait Time 1
7–7 Wait Time 2
7–8 Wait-Time Student Payoffs
7–9 Wait-Time Teacher Payoffs
7–10 Prompting Techniques
7–11 Interactive Questioning
7–12 Teacher Idiosyncrasies
7–13 Review of Questioning

8. Small-Group Discussions and Cooperative Learning

Overview

Chapter 8 provides a thorough introduction to the classroom uses of six types of small-group discussions and cooperative learning. Successful acquisition of the instructional strategies associated with group learning gives teachers a powerful teaching tool. Conversely, poor discussion techniques produce classroom disasters. Because the processes are so important, the chapter is designed to provide your students with (1) a conceptual base, and (2) definitive teaching guidelines.

Part 1 illustrates process objectives and their role in instruction. Critical to the success of small-group discussions is that students meet prerequisite learning outcomes. Facilitating a discussion is a thoroughly planned process and we amply enunciate that point.

Part 2 provides a set of examples of six basic discussion types. There are many more, but for an introduction, these are very adequate.

Part 3 is devoted to the Cooperative Learning Model. We view co-op learning as an extension of small-group discussions. It is important for your students to master the conceptual basis of group learning, especially for cooperative learning. Cooperative learning may be so different from your students' experiences that a visit to a classroom using cooperative learning is suggested. Or, bring in some teachers who can describe how it works in their classes.

Part 4 gives the reader a few tips on how to initiate small-group discussions in the classroom and how important it is to stress "listening skills."

We actually teach each small-group discussion type with **the** method described in this chapter. Topics are selected from the chapter or from local or state issues. We model the guidelines suggested for specific discussion types. We also have our students analyze each discussion. Possibly the most meaningful part of the activity is the evaluation phase. Teachers are not accustomed to evaluating group *processes,* thus first-hand experience with process evaluation is crucial to experiential learning.

Relevant Student Activities

1. Small groups can be developed on the basis of social skills, academic skills, or interests (or a combination of these). Divide the class into 5 groups of 4 students each, then use Activity Sheet 8A (class list) and have each group give a rationale for planning students into the groups.

2. Choose a section or chapter from a textbook in your content area. (Or choose a topic or concept from your content area.) Develop 5 questions that would generate a stimulating class discussion. Use one of these questions to develop a discussion with peers.

3. Design a week's lesson using cooperative learning techniques as teaching tools.

4. Design a small-group activity designed to stimulate student interest in learning and discuss each of the following points.

   a. The objective of the activity (what do you want students to get out of this activity?).
   b. The content of the activity: the tasks you would want students to do.
   c. How would you and/or your students evaluate the effectiveness of the activity?

Activity Sheet 8A

Name	Academic Standing (1=High)	Social Skills	Study Skills	Interests
Rebecca	01	cooperative, patient	works hard to succeed	dancing, art
Del	02	aggressive, hyper	unchallenged	music, electronics
Milly	03	quiet, one good friend	perfectionist	art, music
Warren	04	charismatic, friendly	gets by on charm	people
Marcel	05	quiet, keeps to self	self-starter	reading, animals
Chandra	06	noisy, likes groups	self-starter, leader	sports
Nina	07	quiet, few friends	works hard	reading
Thad	08	energetic, leader	puts in minimum effort	sports, 4-H
Serena	09	fun, lots of friends	perfectionist	people
Janna	10	fun, lots of friends	works quickly	people, sports
Max	11	patient, peacemaker	perfectionist	people, mechanics
Randy	12	hyperactive, aggressive	rushes through work	sports
Marti	13	sense of humor	rushes through work	sports
Sam	14	Cooperative	works by self	animals
Nate	15	blames others	won't take responsibility	grunge rock
Kayla	16	Friendly, cooperative	self-starter	crafts, boys
Mark	17	loud, aggressive	interrupts others	girls
Shari	18	shy, few friends	likes to work by self	romance stories
Jeff	19	quiet, friendly	learns very slowly	animals, 4-H
Bill	20	Hyperactive, leader	learns by talking	hard rock, mechanics

Topics for Class Discussion

1. Define "class discussion." What is the difference between a recitation and a discussion?
2. Identify four other small-group discussion techniques not described in the textbook.
3. Choose a topic from your content area and describe what resources you would need in order to use small-group discussion and activities to teach the concept.
4. Define "cooperative learning." Describe the techniques used in cooperative learning and how they differ from small-group discussions per se.
5. Examine Figure 8.1, page 259 of the textbook. What implications do you infer for using small-group discussions?

Focus Resources

The paper below is one that helps to make all teachers aware of the cultural norms affecting classroom verbal interactions. The author notes that no one teaching method can be used to encourage participation. This is a point that we make continuously in the textbook.

Johnson, E. "Cultural Norms Affect Oral Communication in Classroom." *New Directions for Teaching Learning 70*(Summer 1997): 47–52.

One Internet site has a rather extensive listing of studies and tips on using small groups. Students might find the readings augmenting Chapter 8 to be insightful.

http://www.adm.uwaterloo.ca/infotrac/liblst4.html#small

Student Evaluation Techniques

Qualitative Methods

1. Assign each student one discussion technique to demonstrate via SCL. Provide a rubric or description of how the teaching episode will be evaluated.
2. If a professional development school is being used in the teacher training program, ask each student to videotape a short episode where the student is using cooperative learning. An appropriate rubric should be prepared for grading purposes.

Suggested Essay Questions

1. Describe how you would evaluate the interaction processes of a selected small-group discussion technique.
2. Distinguish between a recitation and a discussion.
3. How could you install a "listening" program in your classes?
4. Describe how you can plan for your initial student led discussions.

Chapter 8 Multiple Choice Questions

1. Process objectives focus on:
   a. Specific behavioral outcomes.
   b. The experience of learning.
   c. Teacher behaviors.
   d. Mastery of specific content.
2. Which of the following is a process objective?
   a. After reading Chapter 7, students will list three causes of the Civil War.
   b. Given a lesson on study skills, students will write out a personal plan for completing homework.
   c. By working in cooperative groups, students will develop written skills.
   d. At the end of week two, students will type at 30 words per minute with 90% accuracy.
3. "Discussion" is best defined as:
   a. Exchange of ideas and opinions.
   b. Teacher lecture and student response.
   c. Assigned readings followed by recitation.
   d. Teacher questions, student response.
4. One advantage of small-group discussions is:
   a. Teacher maintains control of discussion.
   b. Less personal interaction takes place.
   c. Students take more responsibility for their own learning processes.
   d. Topics for discussion are limited.

5. The most important criterion for facilitating small-group discussions is:
   a. The make-up of the students in class.
   b. The arrangement of furniture in the room.
   c. The support of the principal.
   d. The ability of the teacher to develop a "we" attitude.

6. Evaluation of small-group discussions should foremost include:
   a. Written assessment by the teacher.
   b. Assessment by the group participants (students).
   c. Assessment by the leader of each group.
   d. Observations by an outsider.

7. Evaluation of group processes is important because:
   a. Feedback can help students be better participants.
   b. Students are concerned about grades.
   c. All outcomes need to be measured.
   d. Administrators are concerned about accountability.

8. The teacher's role in setting up a class to conduct discussions is best described as:
   a. Noninvolved—the teacher simply stands back and watches.
   b. Plans all the topics to be discussed.
   c. Prepares the class with discussion skills.
   d. Determines the tasks for every phase for all discussions.

9. Since listening is so important when using discussion groups, probably the best teacher technique is to:
   a. Practice the directions first on fellow teachers.
   b. Give directions slowly but refuse to repeat them.
   c. Ask if there are any questions after giving directions.
   d. Call on one or two students to paraphrase directions after giving them, then clear up misconceptions.

10. In group activity, the most important reason for the teacher to be an active observer is to:
    a. Assess and guide individual and group growth in participatory skills.
    b. See that they are recording what is going on.
    c. Select appropriate leaders.
    d. Direct student plans for class presentations.

11. The concept of group cohesion includes the three crucial elements of:
    a. Role, leadership, and purpose.
    b. Purpose, structure, and influence.
    c. Influence, unity, and feedback.
    d. Unity, purpose, and attraction.

12. Three important behaviors for a tutorial group leader to use are:
    a. Questioning, criticizing, and praising.
    b. Questioning, providing feedback, and encouraging.
    c. Questioning, lecturing, and evaluating.
    d. Questioning, evaluation, and criticizing.

13. Cooperative learning groups generally consist of:
    a. Homogeneous grouping of students by ability.
    b. Homogeneous grouping of students by gender.
    c. Heterogeneous grouping of students by ability.
    d. Student self-selected groups.

14. Research shows that cooperative learning:
    a. Improves the academic achievement of students of varied abilities.
    b. Improves students' affective skills.
    c. Improves students' motivation to complete tasks.
    d. All of the above.

15. Evaluation of cooperative learning groups includes:
    a. Individual accountability, group accountability, assessment of group process.
    b. Student evaluation, teacher evaluation, parent evaluation.
    c. Individual accountability, group accountability, class accountability.
    d. Product assessment and process assessment.

16. The role of the student leader in a small group is to:
    a. Organize group activities.
    b. Present main ideas through lecture.
    c. Make discussions for the group.
    d. Assist the group in working together

Answer Sheet and Feedback

Essay Questions

1. Pages 285–286
2. Pages 257, 260–261
3. Pages 282–283
4. Pages 257–258

Multiple Choice Questions

1. b (257–258)
2. c (258)
3. a (257, 260–262)
4. c (261)
5. d (260)
6. b (285–286)
7. a (285)
8. c (282–284)
9. d (282–283)
10. a (264)
11. d (264)
12. b (267–268)
13. c (274–275, 278)
14. d (276)
15. a (277, 280)
16. d (284–285)

Overhead Transparency List

8–1 Advance Organizer
8–2 Elements of a Small–Group Discussion
8–3 Rationale for Small–Group Discussions
8–4 Classroom Environment for Small–Group Discussions
8–5 Small–Group Concepts
8–6 Six Basic Types of Small–Group Discussions
8–7 Characteristics of Cooperative Learning
8–8 Co-op Learning Features
8–9 Initiating Co-op Learning
8–10 Discussion Preparations

9. Higher-Level Thinking: Critical Thinking and Inquiry Teaching

Overview

Chapter 9 provides a detailed rationale supporting the use of John Dewey's classic ideal of problem solving. We illustrate many ways of incorporating inquiry-oriented lessons in any classroom. It is important to discuss and to expand the need for systematic development of student inquiry skills. One assignment won't do it in the K–12 sector. When presenting this chapter, we suggest using the various inquiry techniques so that class members can participate in an inquiry mode.

Part 1 sets the stage for inquiry. Do stress the views on inquiry and those vital 13 processes of inquiry. Constructivism is reintroduced from Chapter 2, but with a caveat. Constructivism is yet a very theoretical model and in our opinion is horribly applied by most teachers and journal authors.

Part 2 carefully subdivides Inductive Inquiry into guided and unguided modes, with ample examples of both.

Part 3 illustrates the difference between problem solving and discovery learning. We close the chapter exploring the teaching of critical thinking and student understanding. These topics are two components of the same concept—understanding. How can teachers best help students to improve their ability to **understand?** Understanding, of course, is basic to functioning effectively both in and out of school. "Thinking" seems almost synonymous with understanding, while a knowledge of the similarities and differences in *how* students approach thinking can be critical in determining *if* and *what* they learn. The short treatment of metacognition might be expanded in class.

Relevant Student Activities

1. Refer to Activity Sheets 9A and 9B to see examples of guided inquiry and unguided inquiry learning. Choose a topic or concept from your area and design both a guided and an unguided inquiry lesson.

2. Choose a topic (concept) from your content area. Develop a lesson plan that emphasizes one of these thinking categories:

   - Critical Thinking
   - Problem Solving
   - Metacognition

3. Think of a controversial issue to present to students. Develop a lesson based on problem solving that defines the issue, explores options, researches facts supporting each option, and culminates in student discussion or debate. (Optional: Try it in a small group or with the whole class.)

4. In groups, choose a problem to solve. This could be a math problem, a jigsaw puzzle, a personal scenario. Have each group member "solve" the problem on an individual basis. Then discuss the metacognitive processes used to solve the problem. Also, discuss the frames of reference or schemata used to solve the problem.

5. Assign several students recently published papers about "constructivism." Establish discussion groups to analyze the papers and the **evidence** presented about its efficacy or effect size.

Activity Sheet 9A

Inductive

Allows individual student contributions, exploration, and creativity.
Allows student to link background to lesson.
Allows teacher to assess student knowledge.
Stimulates interest and motivation.

Examples: Inquiry, open-ended questioning, brainstorming
Emphasizes: Intuition, exploration, details

Deductive

Gives organization and structure to knowledge.
Categorizes details into main ideas and concepts.
Helps students memorize information by making associations.
Gives students a framework with which to understand new information.

Examples: Advance organizer, charts, graphs, examples, pictures
Emphasizes: Logic, organization, concepts

Natural Progression

Inductive:
1. Motivating student interest and creativity.
2. Brainstorming through the generation of ideas and details.
3. Determining student's background knowledge.

Deductive:
4. Organizing details; discovering relationships; making sense of random ideas.
5. Forming concepts.
6. Providing a framework for remembering information and ideas.
7. Providing a framework for understanding new information.

Inductive
Specific Ideas
Details

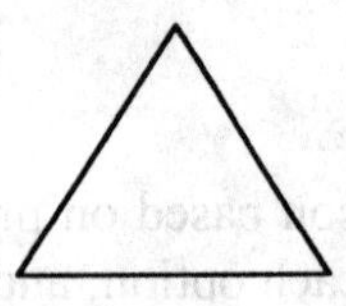

General Ideas
Concepts

Deductive
General Ideas
Concepts

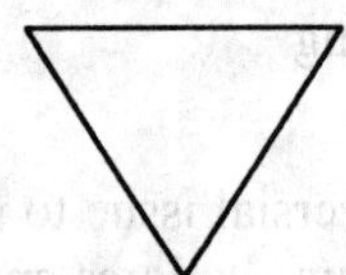

Specific Ideas
Details

Activity Sheet 9B

Deductive Inquiry	Inductive Inquiry	
	Guided Inquiry	Unguided Inquiry
Classify these plants by phyla: bryophytes, anthophytes, coniferophytes.	Tell what you know about these plants in light of our previous study of classification.	Tell what you know about these plants.
Write a review of the experiment stating: hypothesis, apparatus, procedure, results, conclusion.	Interpret the results of this experiment.	Test these substances and tell me what you find out about them.
Describe how the ocean, soil, mountains, and climate affect the occupations of people in Greece.	Tell how the geography of Greece affects people's lives.	Tell what you find out about Greece from looking through these books and the Internet.
Give examples of aerobic, muscle building, endurance exercises.	Watch this video and tell me what different kinds of exercise you observed.	Watch this video and tell me what you observed.
Read this poem and outline its meter and rhythm schemes.	Read this poem and tell me what the author has to say about courage.	Read this poem and give me your reactions.
Read the chapter and find three uses for taxation.	If Europe decided to tax us on all goods that we made, how would you feel?	How do you feel about taxation?
Fill in the chart on cattle diseases, listing symptoms, medication, and seasons.	Thinking of the diseases that we have discussed, which do you think might occur in which seasons?	What do you know about cattle diseases? Share your experiences.
Conjugate this verb in the past perfect tense.	Use the past perfect tense to write a story.	Write a story about yesterday.
Define the following musical terms: sonata, symphony, concertos.	Listen to musical selections and see if you can find similarities.	Find several musical pieces that have a similar theme.
Classify the following elements according to characteristics.	Given the characteristics of these elements, see if you can note likenesses and differences.	Tell me what you can about these elements.

Topics for Class Discussion

1. Compare critical thinking and problem solving by using the following procedures.
   a. Describe the steps or processes for teaching each type of thinking.
   b. What are the advantages of each type of thinking?
   c. Write a paragraph on each type of thinking, giving an example of how you could use each to teach a particular concept.
2. What is inquiry learning? Describe the processes for teaching inquiry learning.
3. What are the advantages and disadvantages of inquiry learning?
4. Choose a topic or concept from your content area. Give an example of (1) a deductive, (2) a guided inquiry, and (3) an unguided inquiry lesson.
5. The class you are teaching is used to deductive, teacher-directed learning. How would you, as a teacher, go about teaching the class critical thinking?
6. Reflect and react to Myron Lieberman's classic statement of the 1950's: Teach critical thinking. That is the mandate of the times. But be careful. Don't criticize anything important. (See *Education as a Profession,* Englewood Cliffs, NJ: Prentice-Hall, 1956.)

Focus Resources

An excellent paper to place on reserve is cited below. The authors provide several episodes illustrating how critical thinking can be approached at the classroom level.

Secules, T., C. Cottam, M. Bray, and L. Miller. "Creating Schools for Thought." *Educational Leadership 54*(6) (1997): 56–60.

The listed Internet site provides your students with a very handy summary of inquiry steps and it tends to validate our treatment.

http://pegasus.cc.ucf.edu/~shr86120/inquiry.htm

Student Evaluation Techniques

Qualitative Methods

1. Assign students the task of demonstrating via videotaped miniclass, how they would plan, organize, and conduct an introduction to a unit that uses guided inductive inquiry. Evaluate by preparing a specific rubric or by adapting the form shown on the third SCL on page 18 of this IRM.
2. Challenge the students to create a two-week unit in their areas of specialization that stresses the role of critical thinking. A scoring rubric or criteria sheet should be developed.

Suggested Essay Questions

1. Describe the epistemological basis for any type of inquiry teaching.
2. To what extent is the constructivist theory subsumed when providing unguided inductive inquiry experiences to your class?
3. Select some topic or concept from your field of specialization. Show how you could use at least five of the 13 processes of inquiry when teaching.

4. To enhance student thinking in the classroom, what skills or attitudes does the teacher need to exhibit?

Chapter 9 Multiple Choice Questions

1. A student of yours sends in an idea to the Microsoft Corporation for a novel way of graphing statistical analyses. This action would be classified as:
   a. An absolute discovery.
   b. An application of guided inductive discovery.
   c. A relative discovery.
   d. A simulated discovery.

2. Citing his criteria for problem solving, you agree that John Dewey had a sound theory regarding the subject. Which criterion would support your decision from the list below?
   a. Problems are only relevant to the student.
   b. Problems are only relevant to the teacher and the broader culture.
   c. Problems should be significant to the culture as well as the learner.
   d. The type of problems being solved are unimportant; it is the *process* that is important.

3. In unguided inquiry:
   a. The students have little control of the learning process.
   b. The teacher provides the basic lesson structure, but lets students draw their own conclusions.
   c. The students provide the basic lesson structure and draw their own conclusions.
   d. The teacher maintains control of the learning process throughout the entire lesson.

4. An example of a guided inquiry lesson would be:
   a. The teacher gives students some paints and asks them to find out everything they can about color.
   b. The teacher gives the students the three primary colors and asks them to discover how to make the secondary colors of green, orange, purple.
   c. The teacher lectures on primary and secondary colors, showing examples.
   d. The teacher tells the students how to make secondary colors; the students make the colors as the teacher gives directions.

5. An example of an unguided inquiry lesson would be:
   a. The teacher gives students some paint and asks them to find out everything they can about color.
   b. The teacher gives the students the three primary colors and asks them to discover how to make the secondary colors of green, orange, purple.
   c. The teacher lectures on primary and secondary colors, showing examples.
   d. The teacher tells the students how to make secondary colors; the students make the colors as the teacher gives directions.

6. Inquiry-based lessons:
   a. Tend to emphasize process over content.
   b. Take less time to complete.
   c. Result in more material being covered.
   d. Emphasize details over concepts.

7. Inductive learning:
   a. Can only be used in scientific and experimental fields of study.
   b. Can be used in English, but not in theater.
   c. Has no place in physical education classes.
   d. Can be used in any field of study.

8. The teacher's role in conducting or facilitating an inquiry lesson is that of:
   a. Social Worker: to address the individual needs of students.
   b. Greater Clarifier: to help learners define problem and processes.
   c. Information Giver: to lecture students on important concepts.
   d. Problem Solver: to tell students how to solve problems.
9. Which statement below is NOT characteristic of inductive inquiry teaching?
   a. Teachers encourage a number of responses from students.
   b. Students must be taught process associated with inquiry.
   c. Solutions to the problems should be found in student textbooks.
   d. Students at all levels of learning can benefit from inquiry.
10. Which set of truncated steps is the most appropriate for problem-solving or inquiry?
   a. Make generalizations, collect data, change conclusions.
   b. Collect data, make hypotheses, define terms.
   c. Define problem, collect data, evaluate data.
   d. Establish limits, fit data to hypotheses, make conclusions.
11. Which questioning techniques would be most appropriate for most inquiry lessons?
   a. Ask divergent, analysis, evaluative questions.
   b. Use questions requiring memory only.
   c. Involve each student in questioning as little as possible.
   d. Seek out those who are intrinsically motivated and ask them questions.
12. If, as a teacher, you decide to use inquiry strategies in your teaching, you assume that:
   a. Inquiry requires a greater amount of time to achieve instructional objectives than direct instruction.
   b. Inquiry will require less time to achieve instructional objectives than direct instruction strategies.
   c. Inquiry requires about the same amount of time to achieve learning objectives.
   d. Inquiry cannot have instructional objectives as it is open-ended.
13. Critical thinking is characterized by:
   a. Knowledge-level thought processes.
   b. Evaluation, judgment, analysis.
   c. Creative, divergent processes.
   d. Intuition, spontaneity.
14. Metacognitive thinking skills can best be taught by:
   a. Using overheads to explain the process.
   b. Having students do individualized worksheets.
   c. Teacher lecture.
   d. Students and teachers sharing thinking processes out loud in the classroom.
15. Metacognition is:
   a. An awareness of one's own thinking processes.
   b. Knowing basic facts.
   c. A lower-level thinking process.
   d. Understanding creative thinking processes.
16. The most important factor in thinking instruction is:
   a. A teacher who understands and practices higher-level thinking processes.
   b. Students who are highly motivated.
   c. Students from a rich experiential background.
   d. Strong administrative support.

Answer Sheet and Feedback

Essay Questions

1. Pages 297–299
2. Pages 294–296, 300, 303–305
3. Pages 293–294
4. Pages 313–315

Multiple Choice Questions

1. a (309–310)
2. c (306–308)
3. c (302–305)
4. b (303)
5. a (305)
6. a (292)
7. d (297)
8. b (292, 304)
9. c (297–299)
10. c (299)
11. a (302–303)
12. a (294–295, 298)
13. b (312)
14. d (317)
15. a (317)
16. a (315)

Overhead Transparency List

9–1 Advance Organizer
9–2 Processes of Inquiry
9–3 Processes of Inquiry (Continued)
9–4 Constructivism/Inquiry
9–5 General Inquiry Model
9–6 Guided Inductive Inquiry
9–7 Unguided Inductive Inquiry
9–8 Problem Solving
9–9 Discovery Learning
9–10 Teaching Creative Thinking
9–11 Teaching Critical Thinking
9–12 One Thinking Process

10. Adapting Instruction for Diverse and Inclusionary Classrooms

Overview

In Chapter 10, we examine emergent instructional topics, including diversity, English as a second language, exceptional students, and gender. We emphasize the concept of public education as a means to noble social ends—for everyone. Since most colleges devote one full course or more to the topics presented in Chapter 10, please consider our treatment as an introduction to subsequent courses.

Part 1 addresses the spectrum of diversity and multiculturalism. We highlight ethnic, racial, physical, regional, and religious diversity. We may be among the few authors who compare the traditional notion of pluralism with multiculturalism.

Part 2 treats English as a second language (ESL) from three perspectives: language diversity, second language immersion, and bilingual education. We recommend examining your state educational statutes regarding these areas.

Part 3 reintroduces exceptional students. Our initial treatment was begun in Part 5 of Chapter 1 of the text, but we do define the term *exceptionality.* The diagnostive-prescriptive model, while oriented toward special education, may be applied to all children who fail to learn a concept. The individualized education plan (IEP) is highlighted from federal regulations and we show how classrooms need to be adapted to accommodate exceptional children.

Part 4 continues the discussion on gender and educational equity that we introduced in Part 4 of Chapter 6 in the text. We amplify awareness of gender bias and misinformation about gender and close with some methods that allow for gender equity in the classroom.

Relevant Student Activities

1. In groups, design lesson plans that address some point of diversity. Present the plans to the class.
2. In groups, develop a resource catalog on the cultural groups in your community. Resources might include: literature reviews, cultural artifacts, speakers, cultural activities.
3. Assign a panel to discuss your state laws, rules, and regulations that govern ESL.
4. Invite your ESL specialist to address the class on how to help non-English-speaking students toward higher achievement.
5. Ask your local district director of special education for actual models of an IEP for class examination.
6. For the Diagnostic-Prescriptive Model, the case study approach has worked well. For optimum results, use several different case studies ranging from crisis problems to normal class learning situations. Divide the class into groups of 4 to 5 students to develop a Diagnostic-Prescriptive lesson. Have students share their lessons in class.
7. Brainstorm a list of skills or activities that we stereotypically think girls cannot do. Do the same for boys. Discuss the implications for teachers and talk about ways to enhance gender equity in the schools.
8. Assign small groups to examine various national reports on student achievement to determine gender differences and at what grade levels they occur.

Topics for Class Discussion

1. Two students in your class cannot celebrate holidays (Halloween, Valentine's Day) because of religious beliefs. How can you honor their beliefs without making them feel ostracized?
2. A student from a nonwhite culture believes in cooperation and sharing as opposed to competition and boundaries. As a result, he tends to socialize, learns by sharing ideas with others, and "borrows" others' supplies without asking. How will you address these issues?
3. One of your students lives in a home with no running water or electricity. The student has hygiene problems which, in turn, cause social ostracization. How will you address this issue?
4. A student from a single-parent home frequently comes to school half an hour late. She has to take her siblings to the babysitter before she comes to school. She says she cannot drop the children off any earlier. School rules say she cannot get credit in your class. What can you do to honor her needs and school rules?
5. You have a student in your classroom with a deformity on his face. Other students tease him and generally refuse to accept him. What will you do to help him gain acceptance?
6. One-third of the class comes from migrant families who do seasonal agricultural work. They are in your class for 5 months only—two in the fall and three in the spring. What would you need to do to help these students both academically and socially?
7. You are teaching in a large city school where 30% of your class speaks languages other than English. How will you adjust your teaching procedures and curriculum to meet the needs of non-English or limited-English proficiency students?
8. Three junior class girls confide in you that the physics teacher deliberately "puts them down" in nearly every class period. What do you do?

Focus Resources

A national debate is raging over the role of diversity, multicultural education, and issues related to the school curriculum. In our opinion, Banks presents the single best analysis of the entire conflict. He skillfully shows the interrelationships of four types of knowledge—personal, popular, mainstream academic, and transformative academic—with school knowledge. A case example using "The Westward Movement" is illustrated showing how multicultural concepts can be incorporated in the curriculum. The debate is raised into a very high intellectual field by Banks. Students will find this paper to be challenging and enlightening.

Banks, J. A. "The Canon Debate, Knowledge Construction, and Multicultural Education." *Educational Researcher 22*(5) (1993): 4–14.

Three other journal articles that we recommend be placed on reserve for student enlightenment are listed below.

Rainforth, B. and J. England. "Collaboration for Inclusion." *Education and Treatment of Children 20*(1) (1997): 85–104.

Weishaar, M. "Legal Principles Important in the Preparation of Teachers: Making Inclusion Work." *The Clearing House 70*(5) (1997): 261–264.

Weissglass, J. "Deepening Our Dialogue About Equity." *Educational Leadership 54*(7) (1997): 78–81.

Below are four Internet sites that expand, respectively, Native American topics and multicultural reform, bilingual resources, inclusion resources, and the concept of "Promoting Human Development" for all.

http://spot.colorado.edu/~aises/aises.html

http://www.edb.utexas.edu/coe/depts/cibilingual/resources.html

http://www3.mb.sympatico.ca/~dhoney/sites.html

http://www.edc.org/

Student Evaluation Techniques

Suggested Essay Questions

1. How do diversity, multiculturalism, and pluralism differ as major social concepts?
2. Compare ESL "immersion" to "bilingual education."
3. Provide one illustration of how you could apply the Diagnostic-Prescriptive Model in your area of specialization.
4. List four ways that you could promote gender equity in your classroom.

Chapter 10 Multiple Choice Questions

1. Diversity is usually defined by:
   a. Cultural, physical, and economic attributes of people.
   b. Race primarily.
   c. Gender, followed by race.
   d. Community cohesiveness.

2. Educational achievement is *least* influenced by:
   a. Racial background.
   b. Education and income of the parents.
   c. Religion.
   d. The community in which a child lives.

3. Religious influence:
   a. Is not felt in public schools because church and state are separated by law in the United States.
   b. Permeates the traditions of school systems.
   c. Prevails only in parochial schools.
   d. Is found mainly in schools located in urban areas.

4. If research shows that a particular group has lesser academic achievement, an assumption might be that the group:
   a. Has less intelligence as a whole.
   b. Has not taken the initiative to solve its own problem.
   c. Does not value education as highly as it could.
   d. Is plagued by economic and social factors that influence academic achievement.

5. Ethnic diversity causes difficulties for educators because:
   a. Cultural standards and values may clash with the standards and traditional values of the school.
   b. Too many ethnic groups cause children to become confused.
   c. There has to be one national set of standards by which to administer schools with efficiency and consistency.
   d. The United States is a great melting pot where everyone shares the same standards.

6. According to the authors, mastery of a country's standard language is probably most essential for:
   a. Nonacademic learning and excellence.
   b. Maintaining inborn intelligence.
   c. Economic and social success within the dominant culture.
   d. Developing one's native language skills.

7. The elements of physical diversity include:
   a. Age, sex, size, handicaps, physical features.
   b. Hair-transplants, body sculpting, and weight reduction.
   c. Affective, psychomotor, and cognitive domains.
   d. Physical, intellectual, and emotional factors.

8. Which of the following statements is true?
   a. Males and females are equally represented in texts and stories.
   b. The female gender is underrepresented in texts and stories.
   c. Research shows that men have better spatial ability than women.
   d. Research shows that women have lesser ability in mathematics, at all levels.

9. Teachers reinforce "learned helplessness" by:
   a. Lowering their expectations for minorities.
   b. Implying incompetence in girls by giving boys more scientific tasks.
   c. Giving fewer leadership opportunities to students from lower socioeconomic backgrounds.
   d. All of the above.

10. It may be cautiously generalized that how we speak:
    a. Has little effect in schooling.
    b. Cannot be measured for impact.
    c. May affect schooling to a great extent.
    d. Has little impact on future earnings.

11. All but one of the categories below is defined as being exceptional. Which one is NOT?
    a. Racial or ethnic group.
    b. Behavior in class.
    c. Physical attributes.
    d. Speech patterns.

12. You have learned about monitoring student behaviors to determine learning problems. Which behavior would be most indicative of a potential learning problem?
    a. Student "A" enjoys working alone.
    b. Student "B" has great pride in work done.
    c. Student "C" is reported to have plagiarized several assignments.
    d. Student "D" enjoys telling you how he has corrected all the errors in an assignment.

13. To evaluate the work being done as prescribed by an IEP, you could:
    a. Require the school IEP Team's consensus.
    b. Have your evaluation validated by the resource teacher.
    c. Complete prescribed federal forms.
    d. Conduct an oral examination with the student.

14. React to this statement. "Even though the IEP is team-generated, you are totally alone and responsible to complete its educational requirements."
    a. True
    b. False

15. There is some evidence to support the conclusion that teacher educators:
    a. Show a rather low interest in promoting gender equity.
    b. Do not see gender equity as a problem now.
    c. Are on the forefront of promoting gender equity.
    d. Have stated that gender bias has never been an issue.

16. Test data from the National Assessment for Educational Progress (NAEP) have shown that at grades 8 and 12:
    a. There is no difference in science or math test scores by boys or girls.
    b. The girls outscore boys in math, but do poorer in science.
    c. The boys outscore girls in math, but girls do better in science.
    d. Boys and girls were scoring equally in math, but not sciences.

Answer Sheet and Feedback

Essay Questions

1. Pages 323–324, 330–331
2. Pages 334–335
3. Pages 337–339
4. Pages 345–346

Multiple Choice Questions

1. b (325, 326–331)
2. a (326–327)
3. b (329–330)
4. d (330–333)
5. a (330–331)
6. c (333)
7. a (327–328)
8. b (342–344)
9. d (342–343)
10. c (333)
11. a (336–337)
12. c (337–338)
13. d (339)
14. b (339–341)
15. a (345)
16. d (343)

Overhead Transparency List

10–1 Advance Organizer
10–2 Multiculturalism Equals Diversity In:
10–3 ESL
10–4 Exceptional Students
10–5 Diagnostic–Prescriptive Model
10–6 IEP's
10–7 Gender Equity

11. Assessment for Instructional Decision Making

Overview

Chapter 11 is simply an orientation to the broad field of assessing, testing, and measuring, with an emphasis on teacher-constructed tests. In most teacher education programs, students will complete a full course on the topic. With that in mind, we prepared a chapter that features the awareness and information stages.

The first two parts introduce the professional vocabulary and how tests differ. Part 3 shows how unit planning logically leads to planning for evaluation. This is in keeping with the concept of curriculum alignment.

Part 4 provides the basics on constructing objective tests, while Part 5 focuses on constructing performance assessments. We close in Part 6 with a practical discussion about grading. With several states now using "high stakes" testing, prospective teachers cannot learn too much about this vital technical component of teaching.

Relevant Student Activities

1. Assign a task group the mission of determining how your state board of education or legislature has established the state-wide testing program.
2. Obtain a copy of the latest report from the National Assessment for Educational Progress (NAEP). Analyze the types of questions asked of 4th, 8th, and 12th graders.
3. In a class "clinic" establish small groups to create relevant rubrics that the students can use when teaching.
4. Invite a teacher who uses well-developed unit plans to discuss how the assessment parts are integrated in the plan.

Topics for Class Discussion

1. Grading is never easy or pleasant. Organize the class into discussion groups with the following charge. Determine a letter grade to indicate student achievement at the end of a term. Be sure to include the following factors:
   a. Which student behaviors, products, and performances will be included? Omitted? Why? What weight will you assign to each?
   b. How will achievement be monitored and recorded during the grading period?
   c. How will you determine a letter grade that accurately reflects the weightings above?
   d. How will you keep students informed of their progress during the grading term?
2. To what extent should grades be raised or lowered because of either good or bad class behavior?
3. What criteria should be established in advance for grading essay questions?
4. How will the use of portfolios change teacher assessment practices?

Focus Resources

The journal paper below provides a quick summary of classroom assessment methods, with examples. It might be used as required reading.

Marzano, R. J. "An Array of Strategies for Classroom Teachers." *Momentum 28*(2) (1997): 6–10.

An interesting Internet site with 15 developed interdisciplinary curriculum units can provide your students with a wealth of test alignment ideas.

http://aelliot.ael.org/pnp/pnp013.html

Student Evaluation Techniques

Suggested Essay Questions

1. Curriculum alignment is a major concept in this text. In no more than one-half page, explain the term and its relevance to assessment.
2. Student performances can be effectively monitored and assessed with rating scales, checklists, and anecdotal records. In no more than one-half page for each of the three topics, explain what each is and how each is best used as an assessment tool.
3. Test questions can be labeled as either "objective" or "performance." Explain the characteristics and best uses of each. Limit your response to one-half page per type.
4. Planning is a major step in test construction. Explain why this is so and describe the steps you would take in planning a unit test. Limit your response to one page.

Chapter 11 Multiple Choice Questions

1. Each of the following is an example of an objective test item type *except*:
   a. Multiple choice.
   b. Interpretive exercise.
   c. Rubric.
   d. Matching quiz.
2. Which objective item is usually considered the most useful by test writers?
   a. Matching.
   b. Restricted essay.
   c. Short answer.
   d. Multiple choice.
3. The objective item most difficult to score accurately is the:
   a. Short answer.
   b. Matching.
   c. True-False.
   d. Multiple choice.
4. Higher-level thinking skills are best assessed by which item type?
   a. Multiple choice.
   b. Extended-response essay.
   c. Interpretive exercise.
   d. Short answer.

5. Carefully planned portfolios of student work exhibit several characteristics. Which of the following is NOT one of those characteristics?
   a. An emphasis upon student errors.
   b. Student access to the portfolio.
   c. A focus upon products as evidence of progress.
   d. Objectives determined jointly by teacher and students.

6. Of the objective test items, which is the most useful for assessing complex thinking processes?
   a. Matching.
   b. Interpretive exercise.
   c. Restricted-response essay.
   d. Short answer.

7. The "inclusion principle" in determining grades refers to:
   a. Special populations.
   b. Omitting some students from the process.
   c. Including both objective and essay tests.
   d. Never having too much data.

8. Of the items listed below, which one would many teachers be reluctant to include in determining achievement grades?
   a. Unit tests.
   b. Weekly quizzes.
   c. Conduct.
   d. Homework.

9. Several characteristics of anecdotal record-keeping are listed below. Which one does *not* belong?
   a. Record primarily negative behaviors.
   b. Keep record brief.
   c. Don't make judgments on a single occurrence.
   d. Make a few observations each day.

10. Essay items can be scored either holistically or analytically. *Two* responses below show the recommended choices. Identify *both.*
    a. Extended response—analytic scoring.
    b. Extended response—holistic scoring.
    c. Restricted response—holistic scoring.
    d. Restricted response—analytic scoring.

11. The steps in planning a unit test include all of the following *except* one. Which item should be *omitted:*
    a. Make a matrix or 2-way chart.
    b. Prepare an answer sheet.
    c. Determine unit objectives.
    d. Outline unit content.

12. Teachers might make each of the following types of test. Which one would they be *least* likely to make?
    a. Pretest.
    b. Unit test.
    c. Summative test.
    d. Standardized test.

13. The problem with assigning grades is:
    a. The teacher always has far too much data.
    b. The students prefer easy graders so they may show mastery of the subjects.
    c. The teacher often needs more data.
    d. The students always feel a loss of self-esteem.

14. When designing multiple choice questions, the correct answer is hidden in the:
    a. Alternative.
    b. Distractors.
    c. Stem.
    d. No correct response listed.

15. For which type of content is the interpretive exercise the best assessing technique.
    a. When computing columns of figures for arithmetic.
    b. When true-false questions are to be made.
    c. When you need a quick way of assessing knowledge.
    d. When you assign students the task of inferring from a data-set.

Answer Sheet and Feedback

Essay Questions

1. Page 356
2. Pages 377–380
3. Page 367
4. Pages 362–367

Multiple Choice Questions

1. c (357)
2. d (370)
3. a (370)
4. b (375)
5. a (380)
6. b (372)
7. d (382)
8. c (383)a (379)
9. A (379)
10. b & d (376)
11. b (363)
12. d (358)
13. c (382)
14. a (370-371)
15. d (372–373)

Overhead Transparency List

11–1 Advance Organizer
11–2 Basic Assessment Concepts
11–3 Assessment Tools
11–4 Curriculum Alignment
11–5 Constructing Test Items
11–6 Constructing Performance Items
11–7 Grading

12. Becoming a Master Teacher

Overview

Chapter 12 creates a sensitivity to developing lifelong learning habits as prospective teachers. While one could argue that this topic is one for in-service classes, we disagree. All teachers at all levels need to become aware of the best professional arenas that await them as they begin their careers. The enhancement of human potential is what staff development is all about.

Part 1 focuses on individual concerns and the traits of adult learners. Part 2 focuses on the organizational aspects of staff development. Part 3 summarizes the need for continuous learning as a consequence of educational reform movements and the need for more effective schools. The Concerns-Based Adoption Model (CBAM) is illustrated as but one model by which to establish a frame of reference about reforms.

Part 4 shows the many ways that one may seek leadership roles to gain the much-needed experience that is so important for advancement. Further, we encourage new teachers to think systematically about their careers. The planning begins now.

Relevant Student Activities

1. A small group of students interviews a career counselor on tips for career planning that focuses on educational careers. Reports should be given to the class.
2. A local school district director of staff development might be invited to discuss the opportunities and in-service education expectations that the district has for new and experienced teachers.
3. The Stages of Concern questionnaire (from the CBAM) might be administered to the class to illustrate where the group might be concerning the concept of "master teacher."
4. The class could brainstorm areas in which they already know that they will need future education, training, or skills.

Topics for Class Discussion

1. Small discussion groups might explore the question: "How is your learning different or similar to the traits listed on page 391 of the textbook?"
2. Small-group discussions might focus on the growth versus defect models of in-service education.
3. Student reports or even panels might describe the professional development activities available from different teacher organizations or professional associations.
4. A small task group might interview a local school district finance officer to determine the actual monetary benefits that accrue to teachers as a consequence of continued education and in-service education.

Focus Resources

An interesting paper that gives some tips on making professional development more personal are listed in the following paper.

Bunting, C. "Personalizing Development: Six Suggestions for Success." *Schools in the Middle 6*(5) (1997): 9–11.

A very interesting perspective on the delivery of staff development activities is presented below.

Wineburg, S. and P. Grossman. "Creating a Community of Learners Among High School Teachers. *Phi Delta Kappan 79*(5) (1998): 350–353.

Are you interested in developing a reading list about professional development? If so, this Internet site is ideal.

http://eelink.umich.edu/pubib.html#additional

Student Evaluation Techniques

Qualitative Method

Prepare a five-page, double-spaced paper with at least six references about Beginning-Teacher Assistance Programs (BTAPs). All conclusions must be supported. Close with pro and con arguments about BTAPs.

Suggested Essay Questions

1. Select two traits of adult learners and show how they differ from non-adult learners.
2. There are six functions of staff development. Which function would you defend as being the most practical to a beginning teacher?
3. To what extent does it matter to you as a new teacher if the director of staff development holds the defect or growth perspective?
4. What type of staff development would be required to meet the criteria for an effective school?
5. Describe some essential conditions needed to evolve into a "master teacher."

Chapter 12 Multiple Choice Questions

1. Which trait would be most applicable to a Master Teacher?
   a. Holding a Ph.D.
   b. Having classroom experience.
   c. Having attended several universities.
   d. Having read several new books.

2. Long-range career goals are made to:
   a. Provide a focus to your career planning.
   b. Satisfy a state requirement.
   c. Interest prospective employers.
   d. None of the above.

3. Which trait is NOT that of an adult learner?
   a. Enjoys planning for learning.
   b. Is self-directed.
   c. Seeks independent study options.
   d. Seeks the theoretical.

4. The purpose of professional development programs is to:
   a. Help individuals reach higher standards.
   b. Create an environment for learning.
   c. Initiate mutual support.
   d. All of the above.

5. One of the elements of Organization Development is:
   a. To focus on building individual skills.
   b. To expand subject matter knowledge.
   c. To solve problems.
   d. To provide training for subject matter specialists.

Questions 6–10 refer to the growth versus defect approaches to staff development. If the statement reflects the growth approach, select answer "a." If the statement reflects the "defect" approach, select answer "d."

6. The district announces a program to give you a technique that you can use in your next class.
   a.
   d.

7. The district contracts with an outside firm that advertises, "We have the newest topic in American education."
   a.
   d.

8. The district staff development director announces a program that "assures everyone will meet success."
   a.
   d.

9. The staff development office urges teachers to attend "Dr. Smith's Six Steps to Teaching Success."
   a.
   d.

10. The superintendent of schools announces a new staff development program that involves group decision making.
    a.
    d.

11. The "Oral Tradition" implies:
    a. Teachers giving speeches about education.
    b. Administrators speaking to teacher groups.
    c. Individuals calling others for problem solving.
    d. Groups of individuals who set up cliques in schools.

12. It appears that some current school reform efforts are designed to:
    a. Meet global competition.
    b. Create new technologies in the schools.
    c. Improve declining student achievement.
    d. All of the above.

13. The Concerns-Based Adoption Model assumes that change:
    a. Is rather static.
    b. Takes place in spurts.
    c. Is a one-time event.
    d. Is rather continuous.

14. A teacher friend of yours just heard about a new teachers' workshop. "This is just what I need to pick up some quick tricks of the trade," says your friend. The friend may be defined as being:
    a. Proactive.
    b. Reactive.
    c. Theoretical.
    d. A "Gasser."

Answer Sheet and Feedback

Qualitative

A scoring rubric should be prepared by the instructor.

Essay Questions

1. Pages 391–392
2. Page 393
3. Pages 394–395
4. Pages 400–401
5. Pages 402–405

Multiple Choice

1. b (390)
2. a (390)
3. d (391)
4. d (392)
5. c (393)
6. d (394)
7. d (394)
8. a (394)
9. d (394)
10. a (394)
11. c (397)
12. d (399)
13. d (402)
14. b (403)

Overhead Transparency List

12–1 Advance Organizer
12–2 Lifelong Learning
12–3 Staff Development
12–4 Reform Atmosphere
12–5 Being a Leader

Part 3

Overhead Transparency Masters

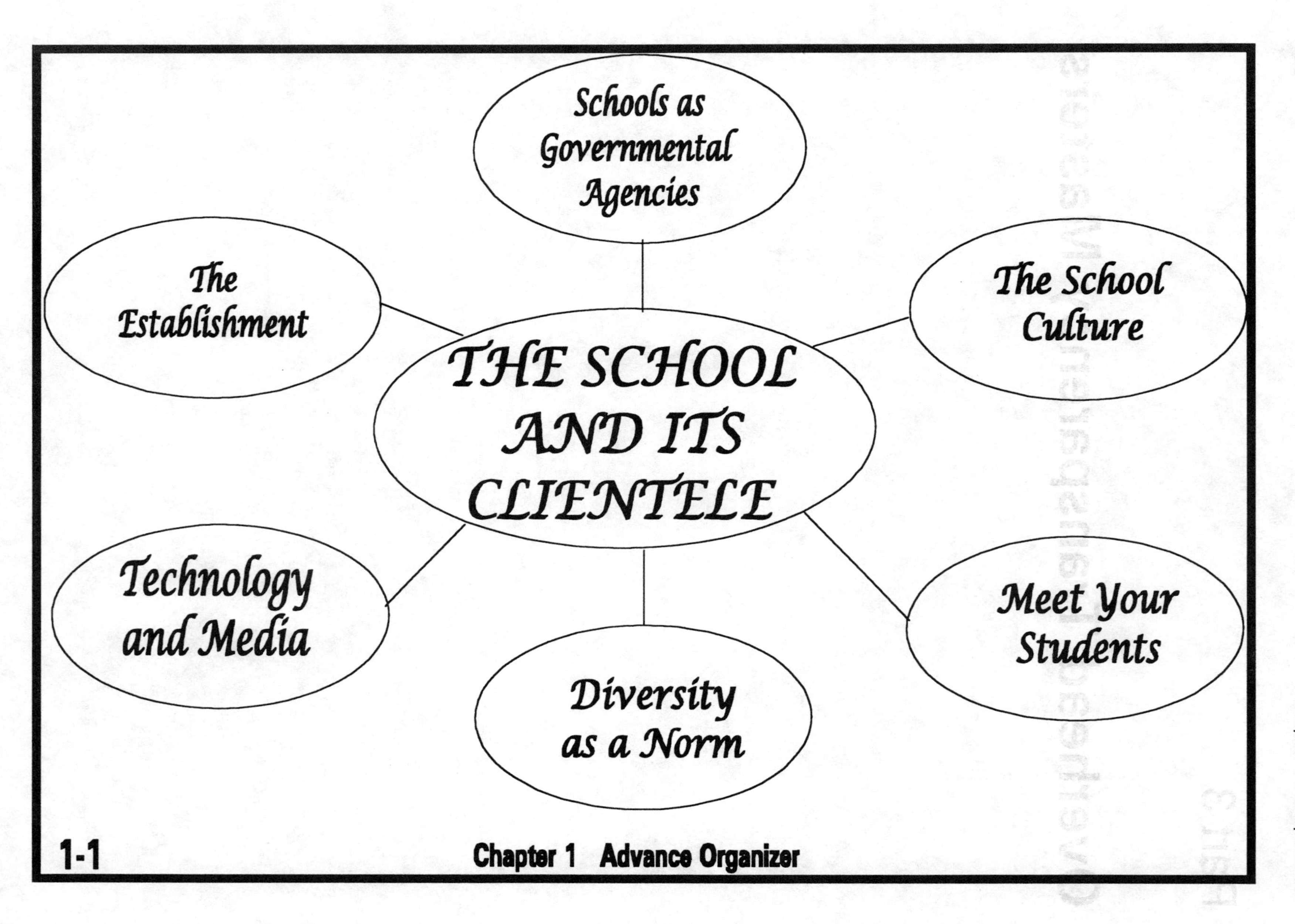
Schools as Governmental Agencies
The Establishment
THE SCHOOL AND ITS CLIENTELE
The School Culture
Technology and Media
Meet Your Students
Diversity as a Norm
1-1
Chapter 1 Advance Organizer

CONTEXTS OF SCHOOLING

- SOCIAL
- EMOTIONAL
- EDUCATIONAL

1-2

SCHOOLS AS GOVERNMENTAL AGENCIES

- LOCAL
- STATE
- FEDERAL

1-3

SCHOOL CULTURES

- ELEMENTS
- INFLUENCES
- INCENTIVES
- LEVELS OF FUNCTIONING
- EXPECTATIONS

1-4

STUDENTS

- AGE AND GRADE LEVELS
- DEVELOPMENTALLY APPROPRIATE INSTRUCTION

1-5

DIVERSITY CONSIDERATIONS

- Socioeconomic
- Inclusion
- Instructional Implications

1-6

TECHNOLOGY

- IMPACT
- PERCEPTIONS OF SCHOOLS

1-7

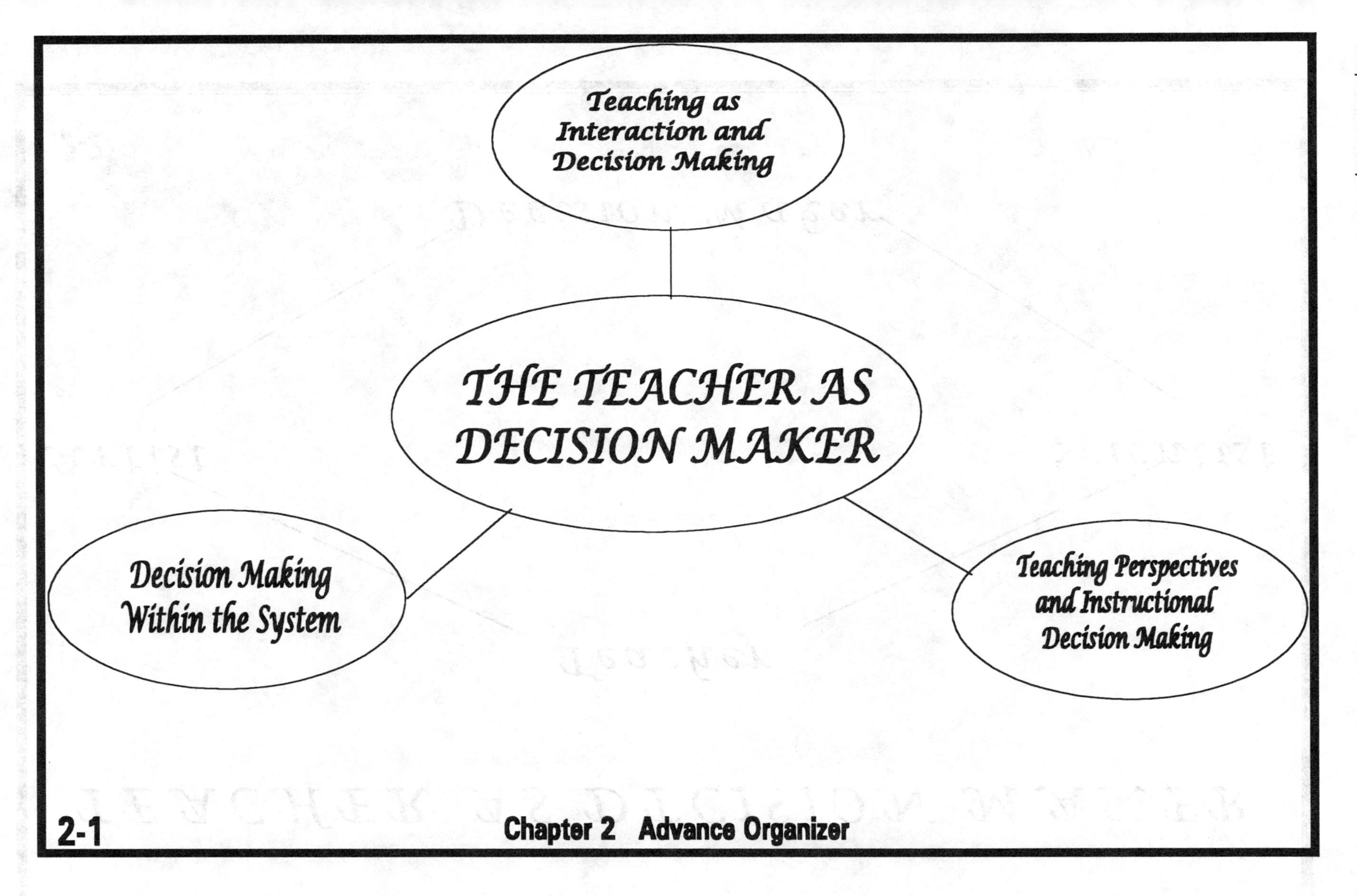

Chapter 2 Advance Organizer

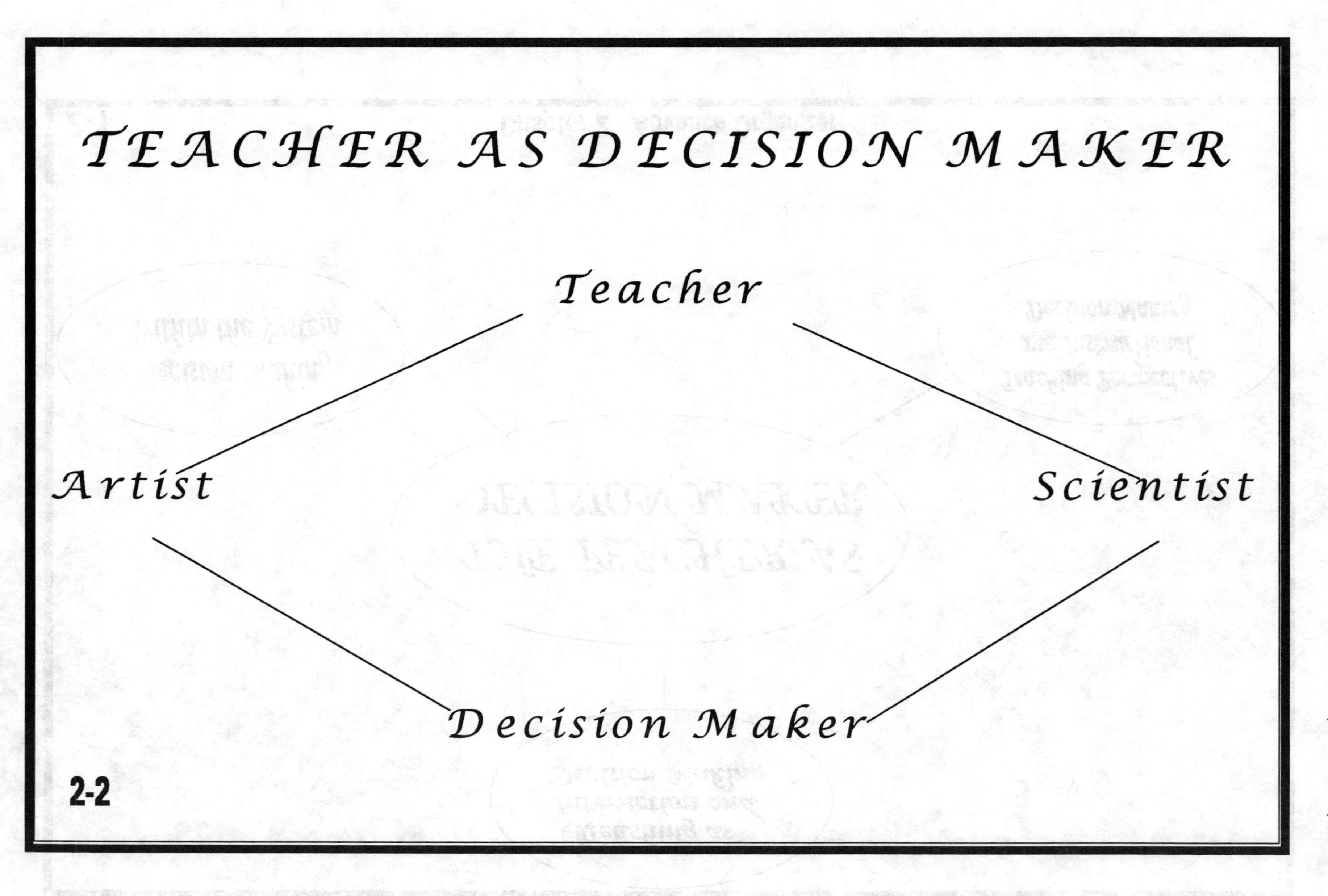
TEACHER AS DECISION MAKER
Teacher
Artist
Scientist
Decision Maker
2-2

MAJOR TEACHING AND LEARNING PERSPECTIVES

- Developmental
- Behavioral
- Cognitive
- Active Learning

2-3

CHARACTERISTICS OF EFFECTIVE SCHOOLS #1

- Positive Climate
- Clear Goals
- Clear Objectives
- Instructional Focus
- Monitor Student progress
- Concerned About Effectiveness

2-4

CHARACTERISTICS OF EFFECTIVE SCHOOLS #2

- Effective Leadership
- Involved Parents & Community
- Student Responsibilities and Participation
- Rewards & Incentives
- Order & Discipline

2-5

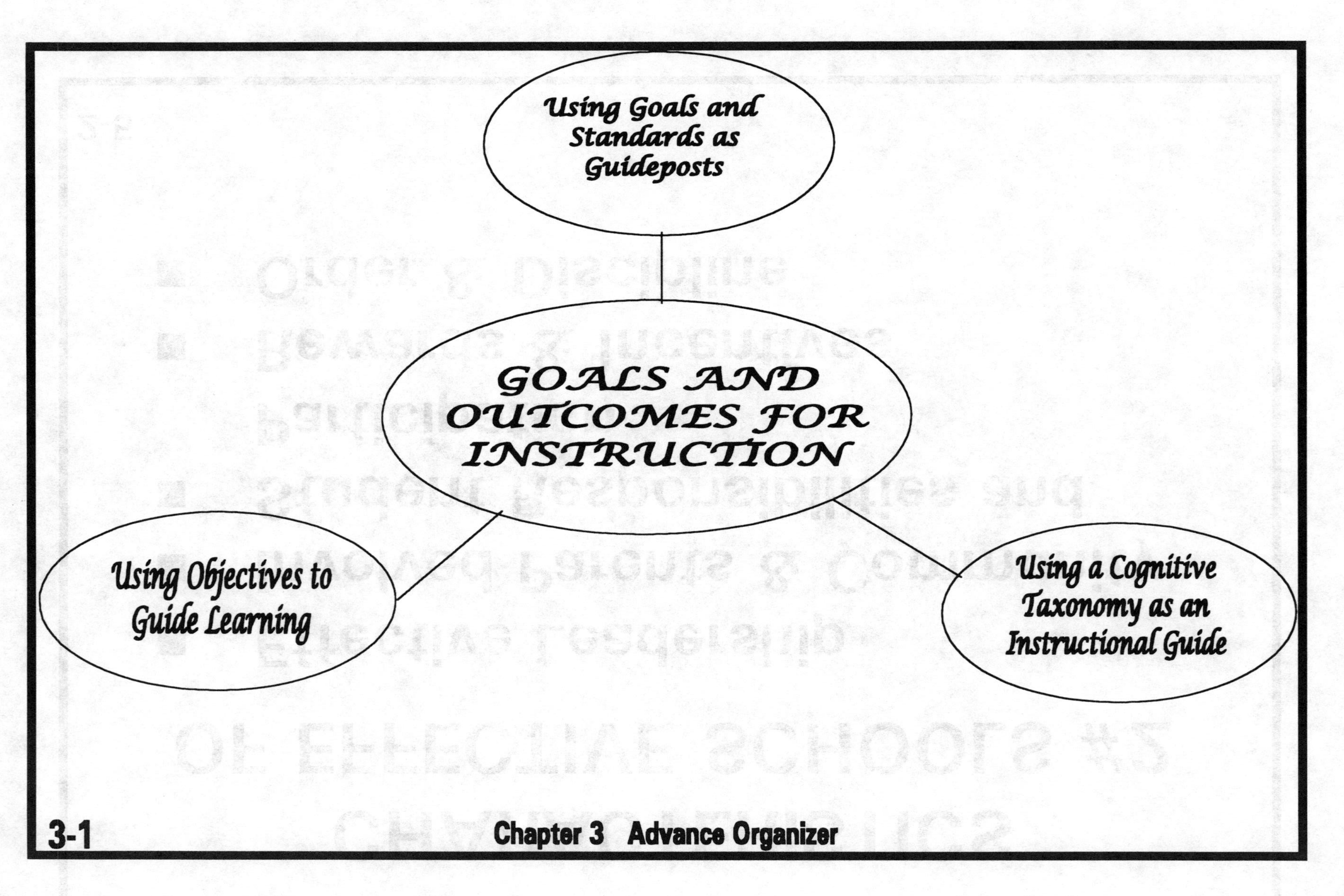
Using Goals and Standards as Guideposts
GOALS AND OUTCOMES FOR INSTRUCTION
Using Objectives to Guide Learning
Using a Cognitive Taxonomy as an Instructional Guide
3-1
Chapter 3 Advance Organizer

GOALS AND STANDARDS

- RESPONSIBILITIES
- DIRECTION FOR INSTRUCTION
- NATIONAL STANDARDS
- STATE AND LOCAL GUIDELINES

3-2

DOMAINS OF LEARNING

- COGNITIVE
- AFFECTIVE
- PSYCHOMOTOR

3-3

COGNITIVE TAXONOMY

- KNOWLEDGE
- COMPREHENSION
- APPLICATION
- ANALYSIS
- SYNTHESIS
- EVALUATION

3-4

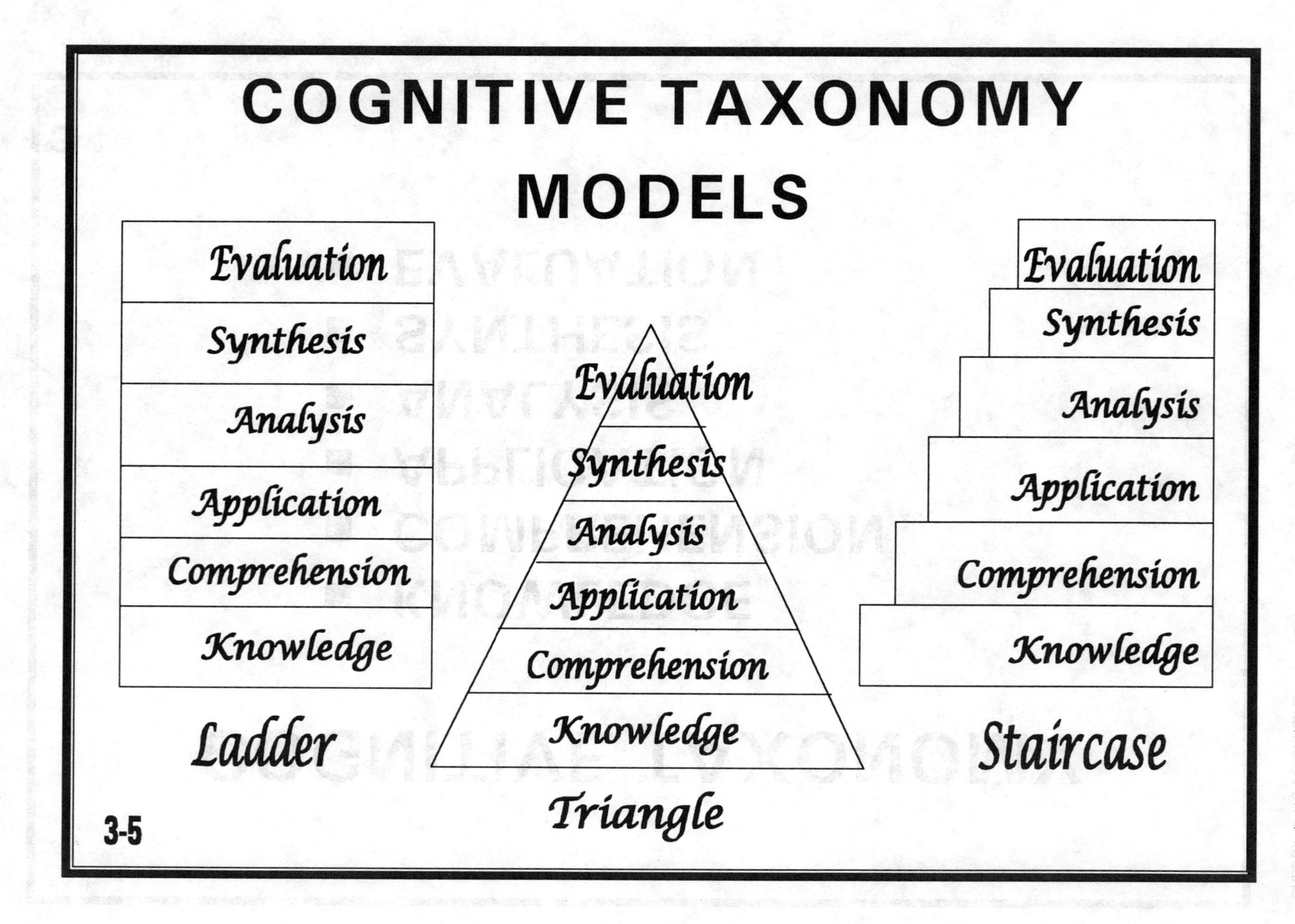
COGNITIVE TAXONOMY
MODELS
Evaluation
Synthesis
Analysis
Application
Comprehension
Knowledge
Ladder
Evaluation
Synthesis
Analysis
Application
Comprehension
Knowledge
Triangle
Evaluation
Synthesis
Analysis
Application
Comprehension
Knowledge
Staircase
3-5

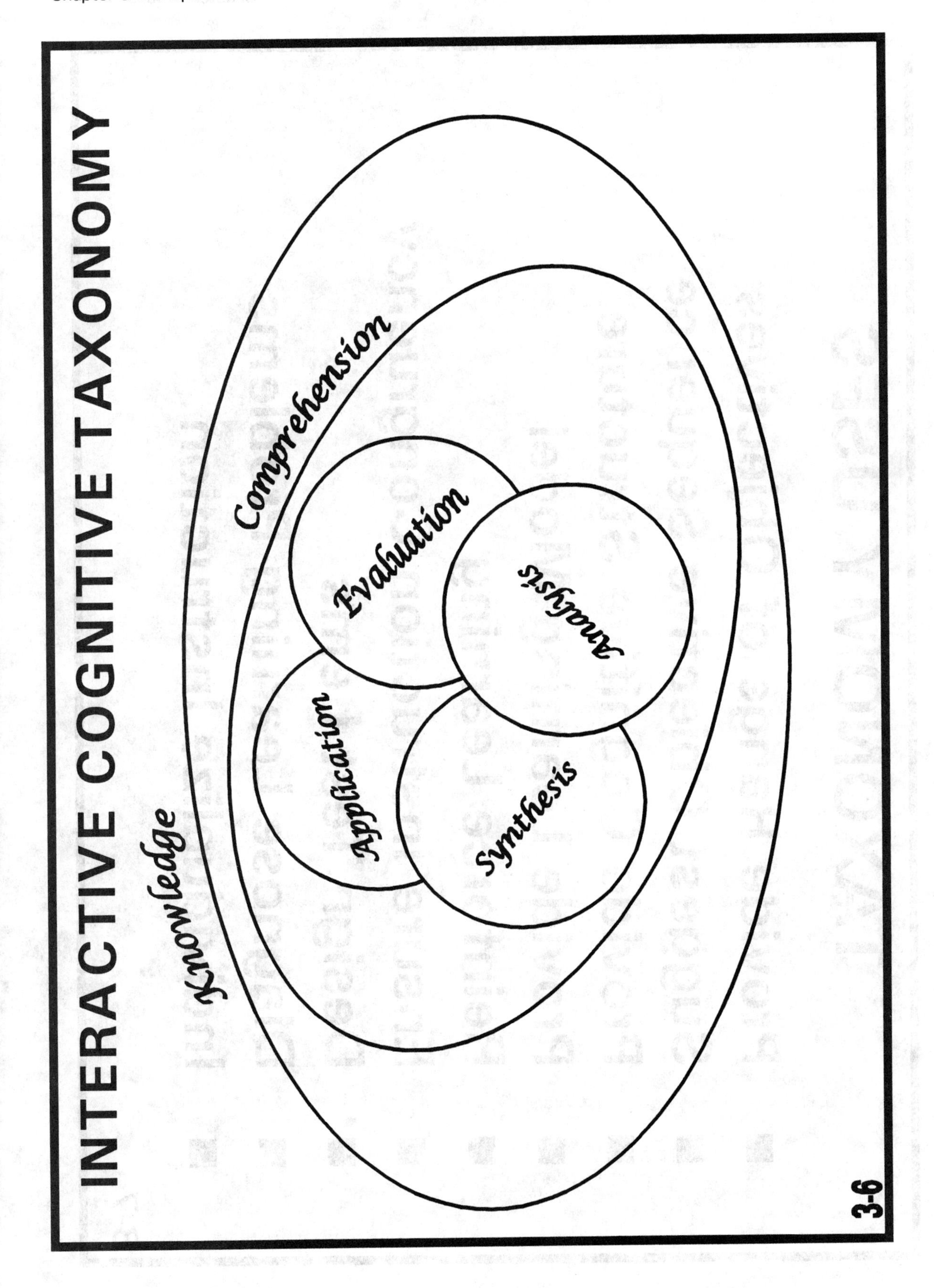
INTERACTIVE COGNITIVE TAXONOMY
Knowledge
Comprehension
Evaluation
Analysis
Application
Synthesis
3-6

TAXONOMY USES

- Provide Range of Objectives
- Suggest Objective Sequence
- Provide Cognitive Structure
- Provide Learning Model
- Reinforce Learning
- Ensure Instruction Congruency
- Design Test Items
- Diagnose Learning Problems
- Individualize Instruction

3-7

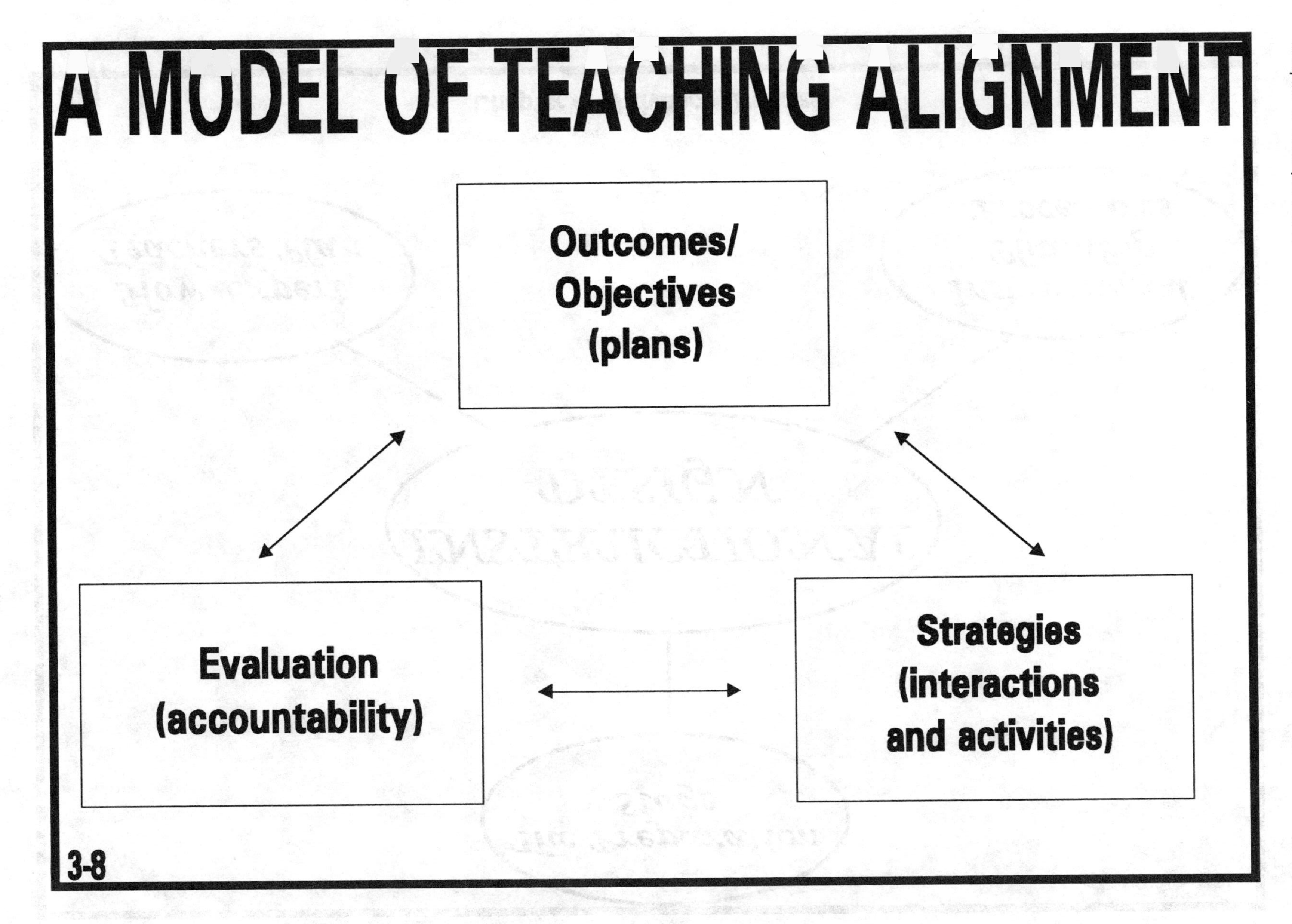
A MODEL OF TEACHING ALIGNMENT
Outcomes/
Objectives
(plans)
Evaluation
(accountability)
Strategies
(interactions
and activities)
3-8

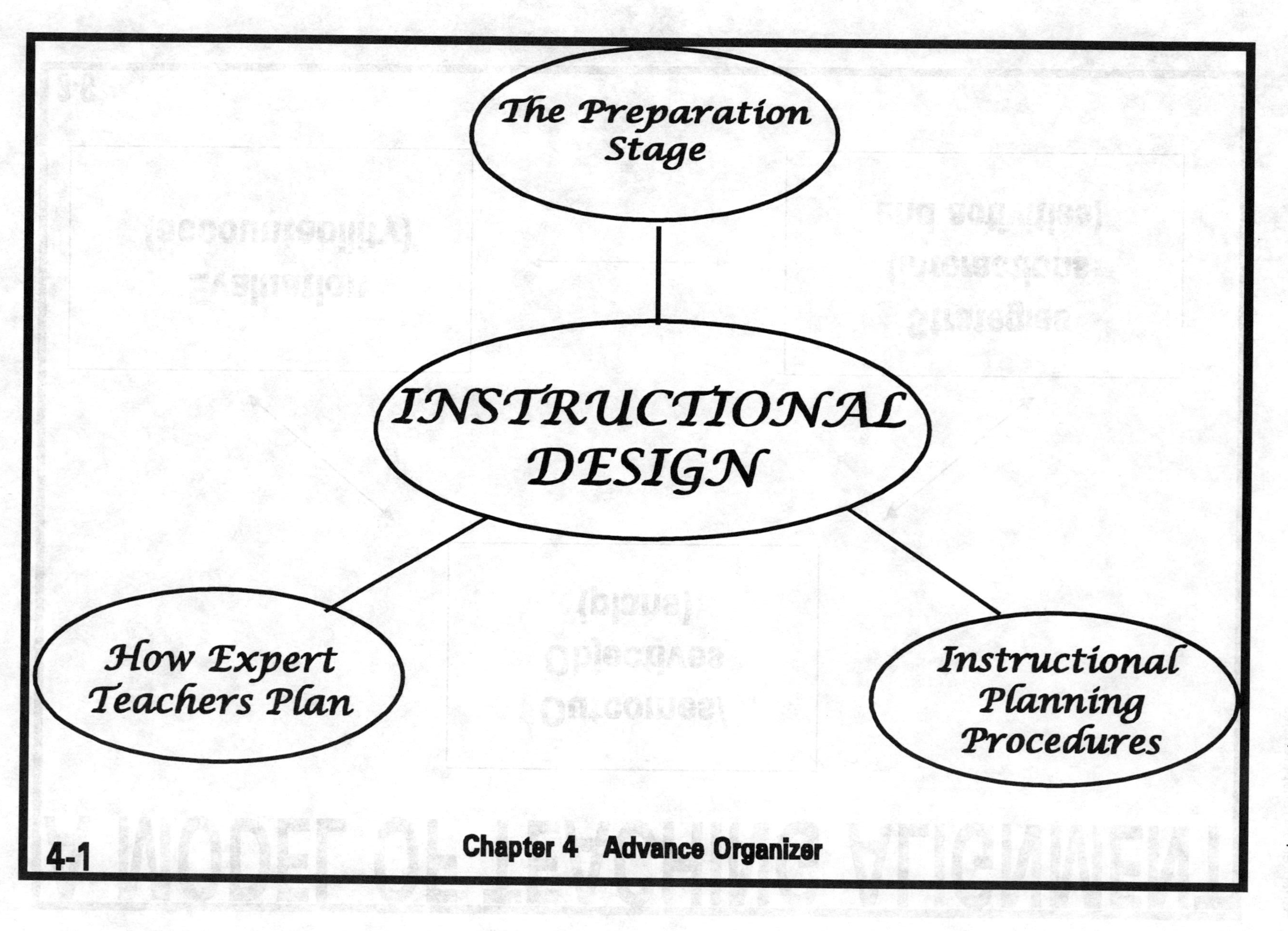

Chapter 4 Advance Organizer

PRELESSON CONSIDERATIONS

- GOALS
- CONTENT
- STUDENT ENTRY LEVELS
- ACTIVITIES

4-2

LESSON PLANNING INFORMATION SOURCES

- State Mandates and Guides
- Curriculum Guides
- Textbooks
- Colleagues
- Professional Journals
- Existing Files
- Previous Lessons

4-3

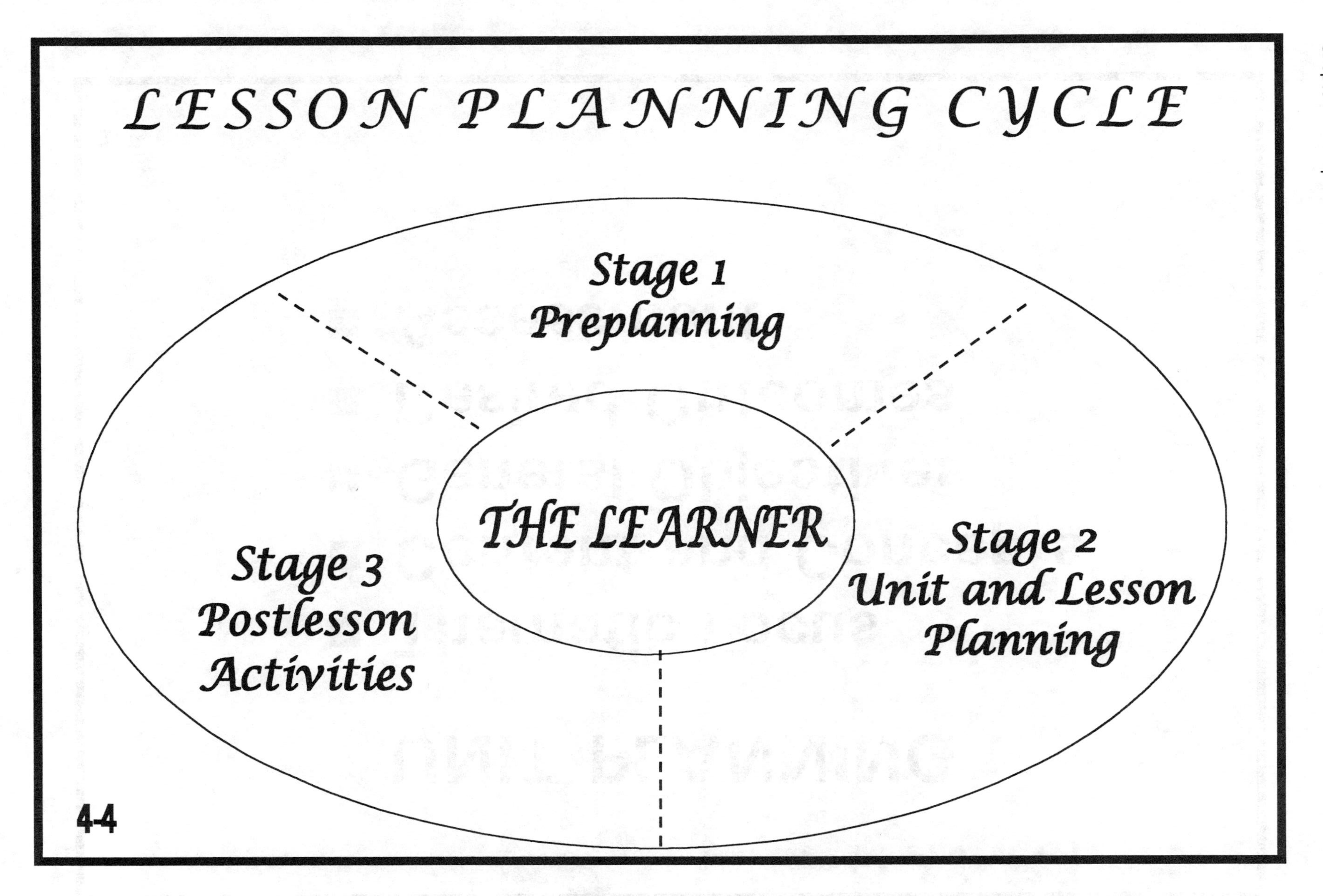
LESSON PLANNING CYCLE
Stage 1
Preplanning
THE LEARNER
Stage 2
Unit and Lesson
Planning
Stage 3
Postlesson
Activities
4-4

UNIT PLANNING

- Thematic Focus
- Content and Concepts
- General Objectives
- Desired Outcomes
- Assessment

4-5

LESSON PLANNING SUGGESTIONS

- Variety of Resources
- Student Participation
- Time to Practice
- Formative Evaluations
- Alignment and Evaluation

4-6

EXPERT TEACHERS' PLANNING

- PLANNING ROUTINES
- REFLECTIVE DIALOGUE
- INTERDEPENDENT PLANNING LEVELS
- TREASURY OF MATERIALS

4-7

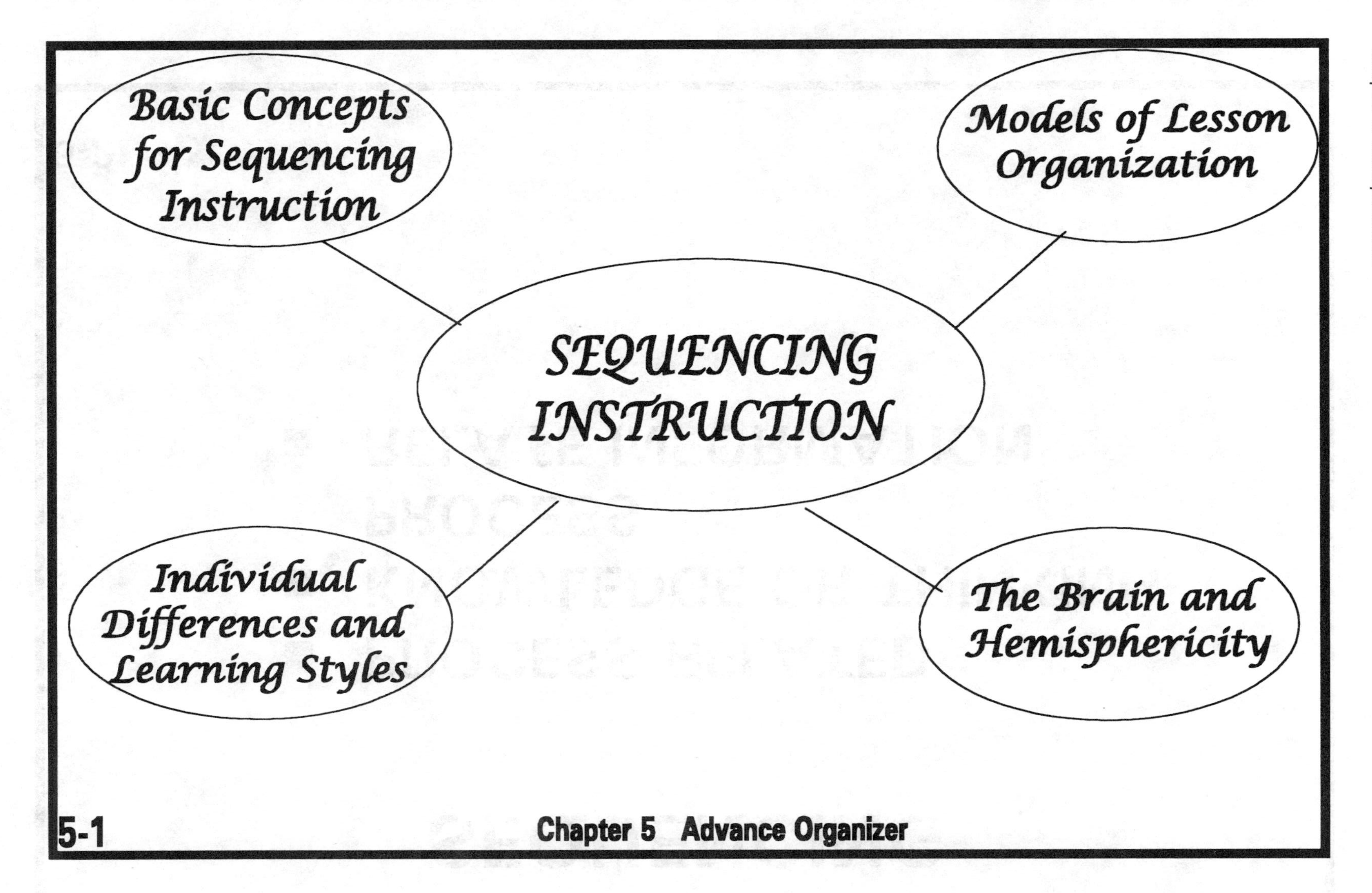

Chapter 5 Advance Organizer

SEQUENCING

- PROCESS RELATED
- KNOWLEDGE OR THINKING PROCESS
- RELATE INFORMATION

5-2

HIERARCHY

- CONTENT RELATED
- PORTRAYS RELATIONSHIPS AMONG ITEMS

5-3

CONTENT FORMS

- FACTS
- CONCEPTS
- GENERALIZATIONS

5-4

PRESENTATION MODES

- INDUCTIVE
- DEDUCTIVE

5-5

MODELS OF LESSON ORGANIZATION

- Task Analysis
- Concept Analysis
- Advance Organizer

5-6

TASK ANALYSIS

- Sequence Intermediate & Terminal Steps
- Select Objectives
- Identify Skill Sequences
- Order Sequences Logically
- Teach
- Revise

5-7

CONCEPT ANALYSIS

- IDENTIFY CONCEPT
- DEFINE CONCEPT
- GIVE CONCEPT CHARACTERISTICS
- GIVE CONCEPT EXAMPLES

5-8

ADVANCE ORGANIZER

- Begin with Advance Organizer
- Progressive Differentiation
- Integrative Reconciliation

5-9

HEMISPHERICITY

LEFT	RIGHT
SPECIFICS	APPROXIMATIONS
ANALYSIS	CREATIVITY
Verbal	Visual
Logical	Nonverbal
Categorical	Spatial
Detail-Oriented	Divergent
Convergent	Intuitive

5-10

LEARNING STYLES

- Cognitive, Affective, Psychomotor
- Understand Problems Differently
- Solve Problems Differently

5-11

LEARNER DIFFERENCES

- HEMISPHERICITY
- LEARNING STYLES
- MULTIPLE INTELLIGENCES
- CULTURE
- FIELD ORIENTATION

5-12

LEARNING-STYLES APPROACHES

- DUNN AND DUNN
- GREGORC STYLE DELINEATOR
- McCARTHY'S 4MAT SYSTEM

5-13

MULTIPLE INTELLIGENCES

- Verbal/Linguistic
- Logical/Mathematical
- Visual/Spatial
- Body/Kinesthetic
- Musical/Rhythmic
- Interpersonal
- Intrapersonal

5-14

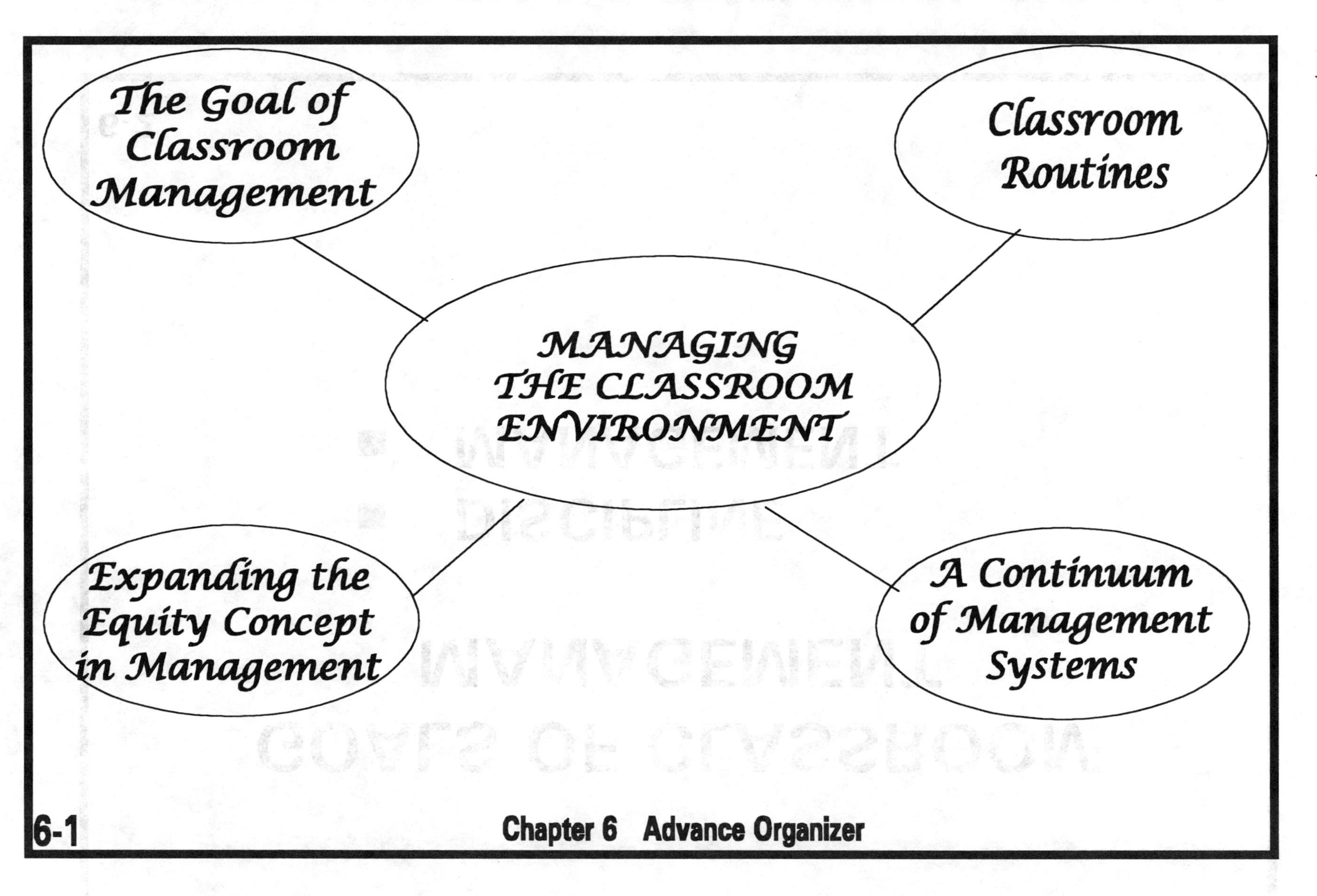

Chapter 6 Advance Organizer

GOALS OF CLASSROOM MANAGEMENT

- DISCIPLINE
- MANAGEMENT

6-2

CLASSROOM ROUTINES

- Plan Ahead
- Establish Useable Rules
- Get Off to A Good Start
- Monitor the Environment
- Provide Clear Directions
- Keep Records

6-3

ANTICIPATED INTERRUPTIONS

- Beginning of an Instructional Episode
- Between Instructional Episodes
- After an Instructional Episode
- Equipment Setup and Take-Down
- Materials Distribution/Collection
- From Teacher- to Student-Centered Activity
- Beginning/End of Class or School Day

6-4

UNANTICIPATED INTERRUPTIONS

- Student Illness
- Visitors
- Announcements/Messages
- Student Behavioral Problems
- Equipment Malfunctions
- Fire Alarms/Classroom Evacuations
- Material Shortages

6-5

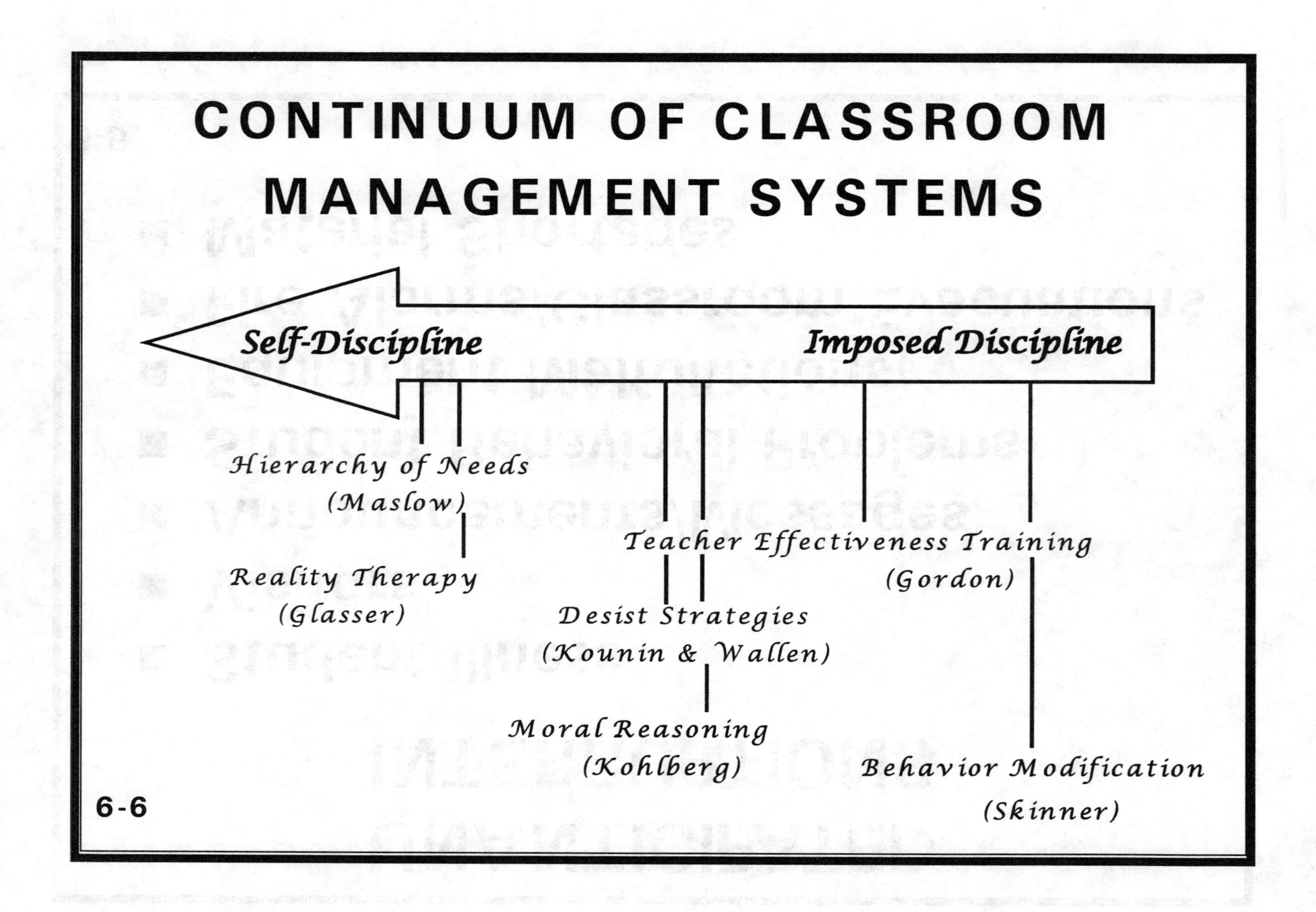
CONTINUUM OF CLASSROOM
MANAGEMENT SYSTEMS
Self-Discipline
Imposed Discipline
Hierarchy of Needs
(Maslow)
Reality Therapy
(Glasser)
Teacher Effectiveness Training
(Gordon)
Desist Strategies
(Kounin & Wallen)
Moral Reasoning
(Kohlberg)
Behavior Modification
(Skinner)
6-6

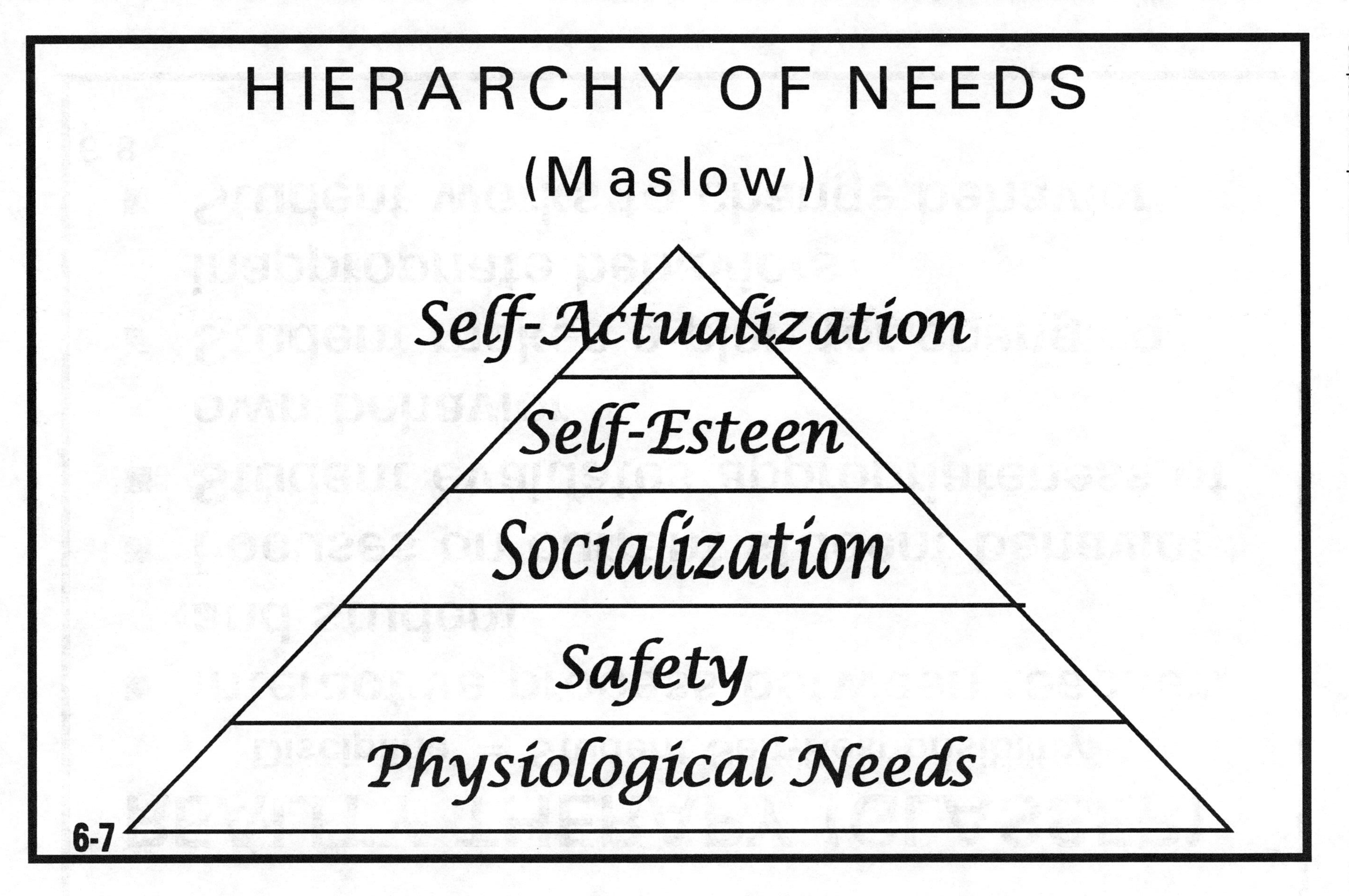
HIERARCHY OF NEEDS
(Maslow)
Self-Actualization
Self-Esteen
Socialization
Safety
Physiological Needs
6-7

REALITY THERAPY (GLASSER)

Discipline = Student Self-Responsibility

- Interactive process between teacher and student
- Focuses on current student behavior
- Student evaluates appropriateness of own behavior
- Student makes a plan for changing inappropriate behaviors
- Student works to change behavior

6-8

MORAL REASONING (Kohlberg)

Stages of Moral Development

- **Punishment as Absolute**
  - Break the rules, pay the price
- **Instrumental Purpose**
  - Following rules to meet one's own needs
- **Interpersonal Concordance**
  - Living up to what others expect
- **Law and Order**
  - *Right* equals contributing to social system
- **Social Contract**
  - Human rights supercede social system
- **Universal Ethical Principle**
  - Morality based on individual choice

6-9

DESIST STRATEGIES

Levels of Force

Level of Force	Definition	Strategy
Low	Nonverbal	Glance Headshake
Medium	Verbal No Coercion	Appeal to Child
High	Verbal, Nonverbal Coercion	Raise Voice Threaten Punish

6-10

DESIST STRATEGIES
Type

Type	Definition	Strategy
Public	Noticed by Most of the Class	Act or Speak Out
Private	Noticed by Only a Few Children	Use Unobtrusive Actions

6-11

BEHAVIOR MODIFICATION

- Pinpoint Exact Behavior You Want to Change
- Chart Baseline Behavior
- Intervene: Implement a Plan for Changing the Behavior
- Reverse: Remove Interventions
- Reintervene

6-12

EFFECTIVE CLASSROOM MANAGEMENT

- ACCENTUATE POSITIVE
- IDENTIFY APPROPRIATE BEHAVIORS
- START SMALL
- BE CONSISTENT

6-13

ISSUES IN MANAGEMENT

- Gender and Equity Issues
- Complex Instructional Environments
- Tracking
- Parental Involvement
- Referrals/Case Management
- Alcohol and Drug Management
- Records Management

6-14

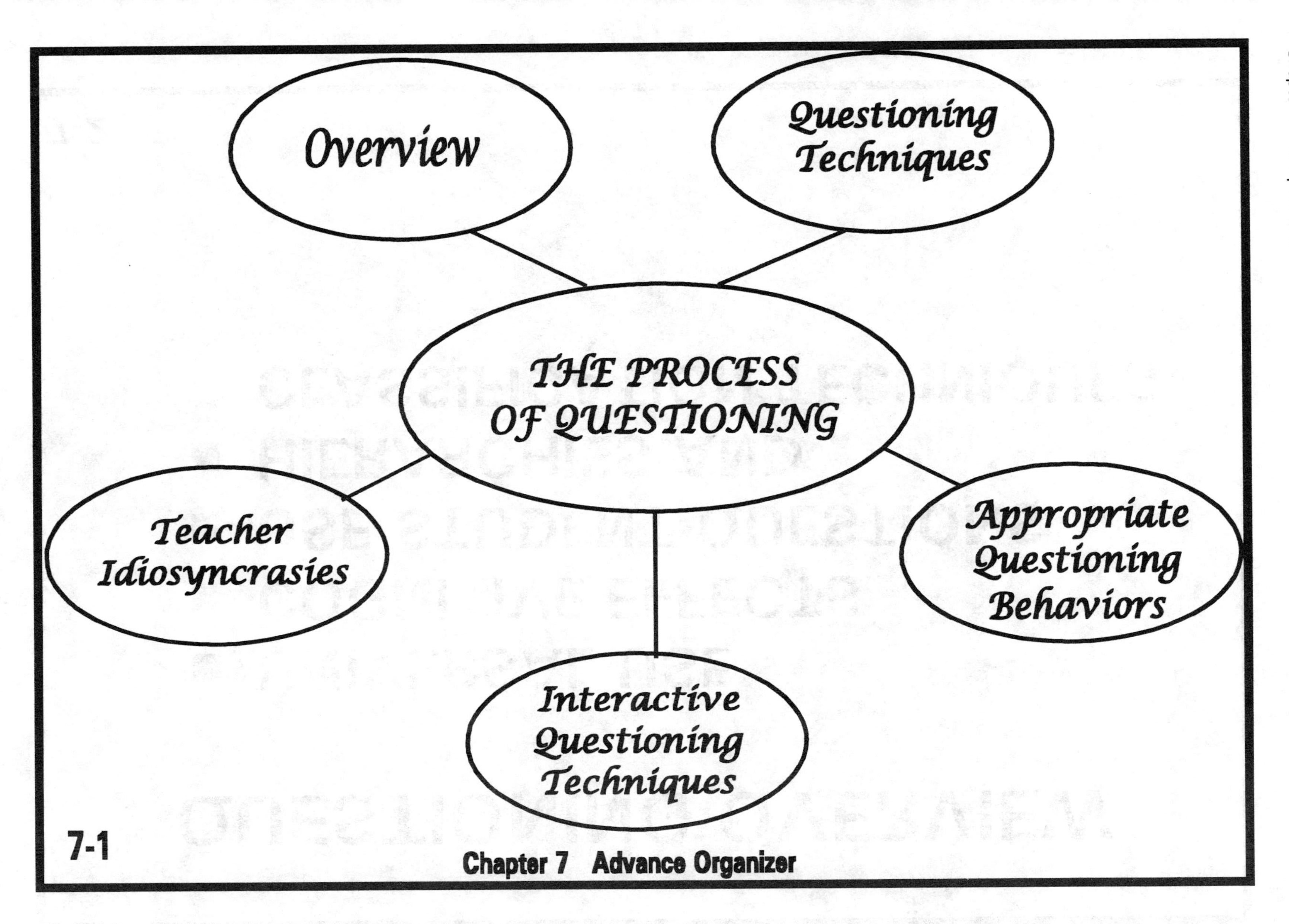

Chapter 7 Advance Organizer

QUESTIONING OVERVIEW

- UNIVERSAL USE
- COGNITIVE EFFECTS
- USE STUDENT QUESTIONS
- HIERARCHIES AND CLASSIFICATION TECHNIQUES

7-2

BASIC QUESTIONING CATEGORIES

- CONVERGENT
- DIVERGENT
- EVALUATIVE

7-3

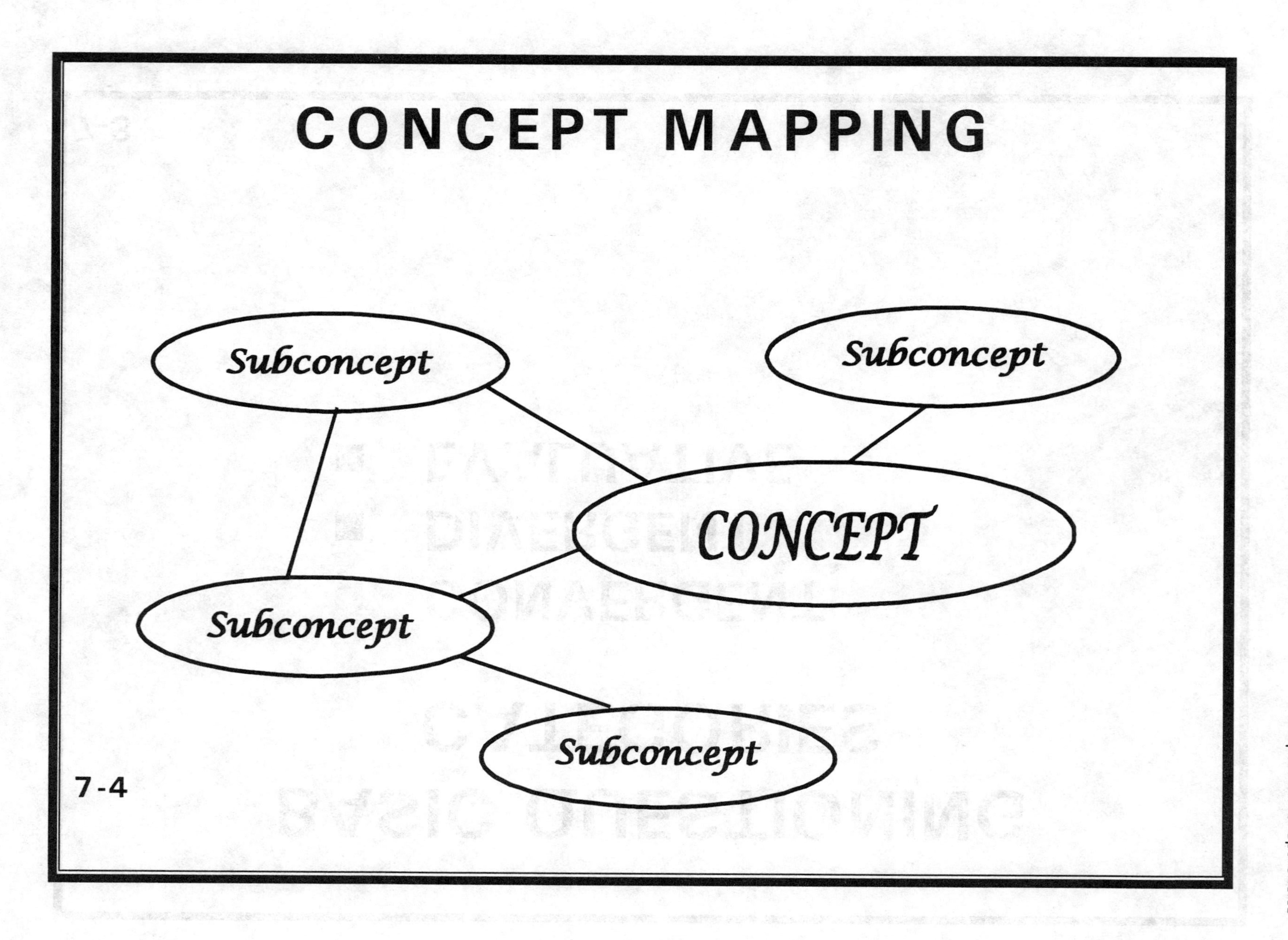
CONCEPT MAPPING
Subconcept
Subconcept
CONCEPT
Subconcept
Subconcept
7-4

QUESTIONING CONSIDERATIONS

- FRAMING QUESTIONS— WAIT TIME
- PROMPTING
- HANDLING INCORRECT RESPONSES

7-5

WAIT TIME 1

Teacher States Question

Wait Time 1

Teacher Calls on Student

Student Responds

7-6

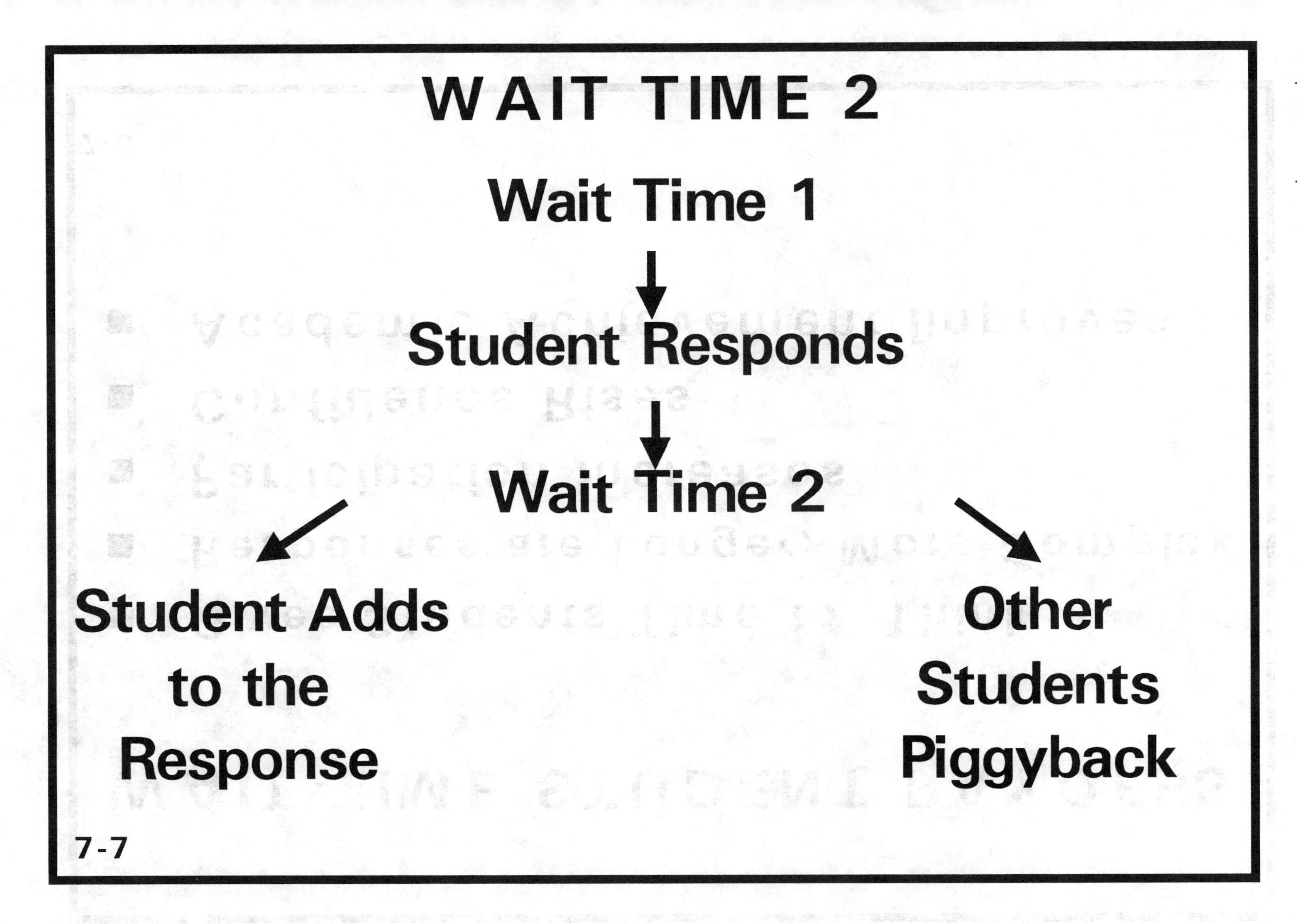
WAIT TIME 2
Wait Time 1
Student Responds
Wait Time 2
Student Adds to the Response
Other Students Piggyback
7-7

WAIT-TIME STUDENT PAYOFFS

- Gives Students Time to Think
- Responses are Longer, More Complex
- Participation Increases
- Confidence Rises
- Academic Achievement Improves

7-8

WAIT-TIME TEACHER PAYOFFS

- Less Teacher Talk, More Student Talk
- Less Repetition of Questions
- More Divergent Questions
- More Application Questions
- More Multiple-Response Questions

7-9

PROMPTING TECHNIQUES

- Reinforce Students Positively
- Let Students Expand Answers
- Avoid Sarcasm
- Restate with Lower-Level Question
- Observe Nonverbal Cues

7-10

INTERACTIVE QUESTIONING

- Promoting Multiple Responses
- Concept Review
- Encouraging Nonvolunteers
- Developing Student Questions

7-11

TEACHER IDIOSYNCRASIES

- Repeating Questions
- Repeating Student Answers
- Answering Questions for Students
- Interrupting Students
- Not Attending to Students
- Selecting Same Students to Answer Questions

7-12

REVIEW OF QUESTIONING

- Use Systematic Questioning Techniques
- Use Variety of Questions
- Adapt Questions to Cognitive Levels and Affective Needs
- Encourage Participation of All Students
- Encourage Students to Ask Questions

7-13

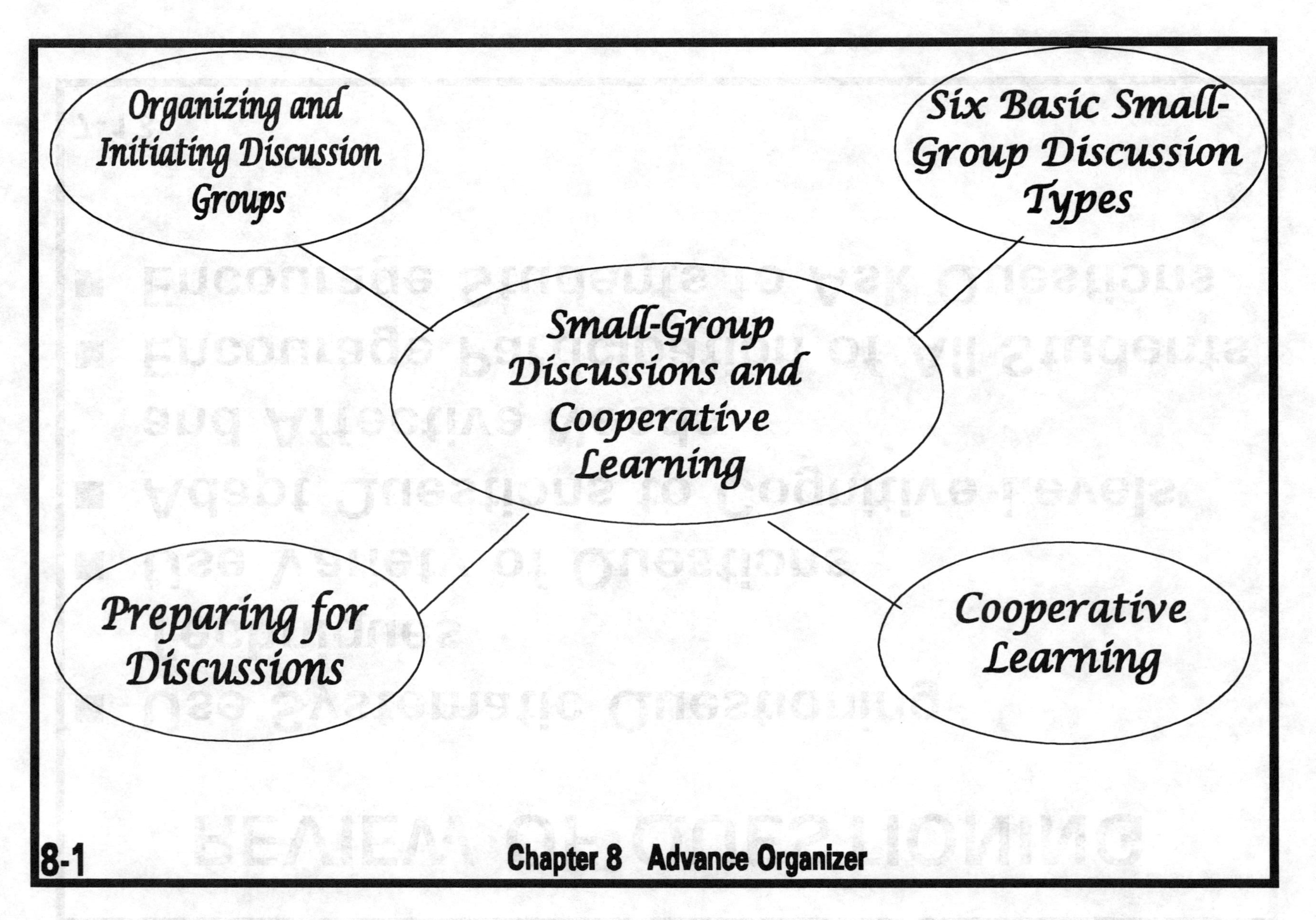
Organizing and Initiating Discussion Groups
Six Basic Small-Group Discussion Types
Small-Group Discussions and Cooperative Learning
Preparing for Discussions
Cooperative Learning
8-1
Chapter 8 Advance Organizer

ELEMENTS OF A SMALL-GROUP DISCUSSION

- 4–8 Students
- Common Topic or Problem
- Exchange and Evaluation of Ideas
- Direction Toward a Goal
- Verbal Interactions

8-2

RATIONALE FOR SMALL-GROUP DISCUSSIONS

- Discuss Relevant Issues
- Honor Diversity of Students
- Utilize Individual Strengths
- Recognize and Solve Problems
- Evaluate Data, Ideas, and Options
- Learn Skills in Leadership, Organization, Research, Personal Interaction

8-3

CLASSROOM ENVIRONMENT FOR SMALL-GROUP DISCUSSIONS

- Teacher as Facilitator
- Student Responsibility
- Supportive Emotional Climate
- *We* Attitude
- Respect for Diverse Ideas and Values

8-4

SMALL-GROUP CONCEPTS

- Interaction and Process
- Structure and Role
- Leadership
- Group Cohesion

8-5

SIX BASIC TYPES OF SMALL-GROUP DISCUSSIONS

- Brainstorming
- Tutorial
- Task Group
- Role-Playing
- Simulation
- Inquiry

8-6

CHARACTERISTICS OF COOPERATIVE LEARNING

- Use Small Groups of 3 or 4 Students
- Focus on Tasks to Be Accomplished
- Require Group Cooperation and Interaction
- Mandate Individual Responsibility to Learn
- Support Division of Labor

8-7

CO-OP LEARNING FEATURES

- Positive Interdependence
- Face-to-Face
- Individual Accountability
- Social Skills
- Group Accountability

8-8

INITIATING CO-OP LEARNING

- Group Selection
- Planning Activities
- Goal Setting
- Monitoring and Evaluating

8-9

DISCUSSION PREPARATIONS

- Listening Skills
- Room Arrangement
- Topic Selection
- Leadership Development
- Feedback

8-10

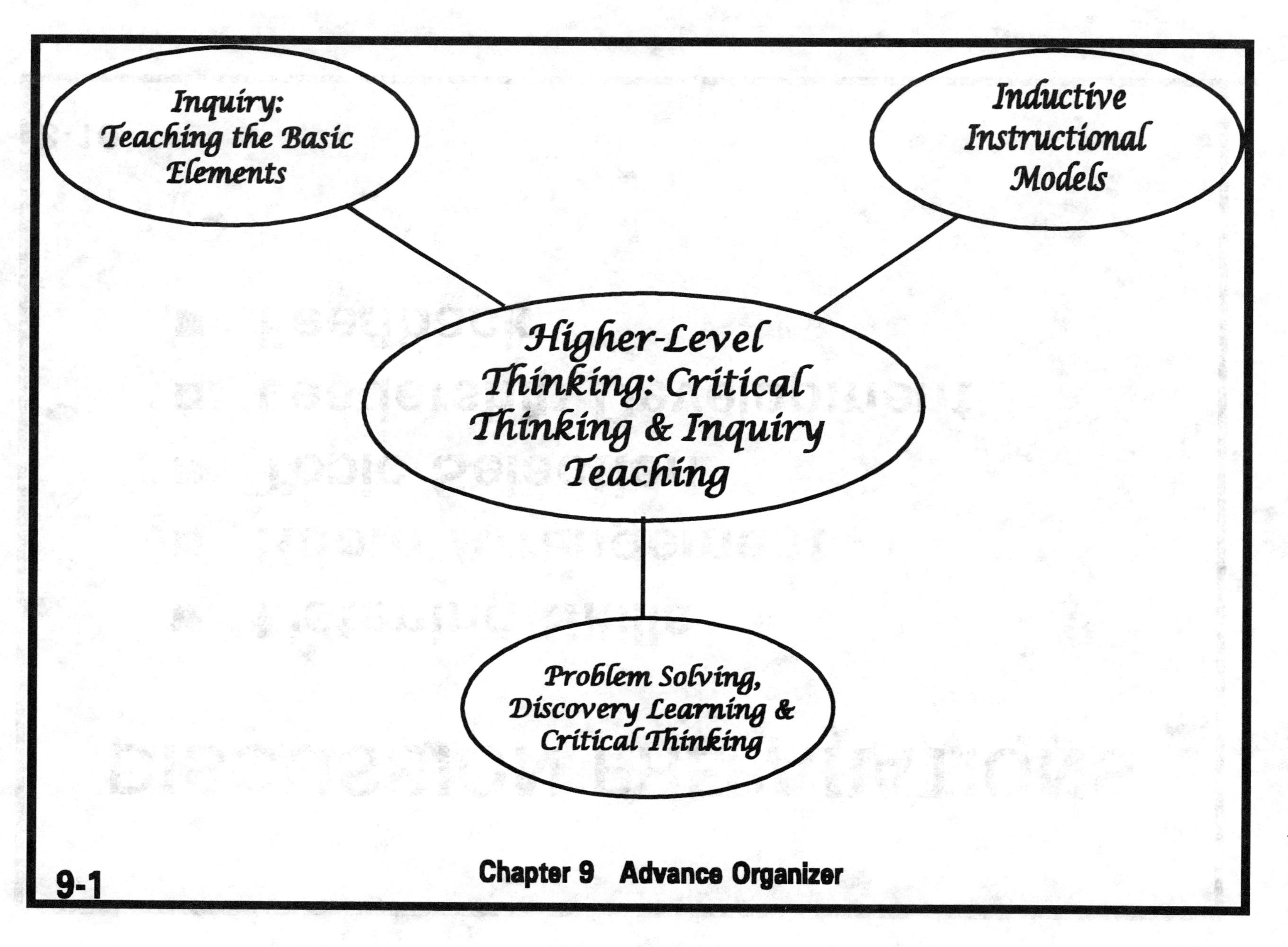
Inquiry: Teaching the Basic Elements
Inductive Instructional Models
Higher-Level Thinking: Critical Thinking & Inquiry Teaching
Problem Solving, Discovery Learning & Critical Thinking
9-1
Chapter 9 Advance Organizer

PROCESSES OF INQUIRY

- Observing
- Classifying
- Inferring
- Using Numbers
- Measuring
- Using Space-Time Relationships

9-2

PROCESSES OF INQUIRY

- Communicating
- Predicting
- Defining Operationally
- Formulating Hypotheses
- Interpreting Data
- Controlling Variables
- Experimenting

9-3

CONSTRUCTIVISM/INQUIRY

- Students Do the Work
- Search for Implications
- Multiple Conclusions
- Justify Methodology

9-4

GENERAL INQUIRY MODEL

- Identify a Problem or Issue
- Set Research Objective
- Collect Data
- Organize Data
- Interpret Data
- Develop Generalizations

Observe (Set Research Objective, Collect Data)

Infer (Organize Data, Interpret Data)

Conclude (Develop Generalizations)

9-5

GUIDED INDUCTIVE INQUIRY

- Teacher Provides Materials
- Teacher Sets Lesson Structure
- Teacher Asks the Questions
- Students Observer, Collect, Analyze Data
- Students Make Inferences and Draw Conclusions

9-6

UNGUIDED INDUCTIVE INQUIRY

- Teacher May Provide Materials
- Teacher Asks First Question Only
- Students Set Lesson Structure
- Students Ask the Questions
- Students Observe, College, Analyze Data
- Students Make Inferences and Draw Conclusions

9-7

PROBLEM SOLVING

- Awareness of Problem
- Definition of Problem
- Task Analysis of Problem
- Data Collection
- Data Analysis
- Suggest Alternative Solutions
- Choose Solution

9-8

DISCOVERY LEARNING

- Absolute Discovery
- Relative Discovery
- Discovering or Learning That ...
- Discovering or Knowing How ...

9-9

TEACHING CREATIVE THINKING

- Use Inductive, Intuitive, Divergent Inquiry Processes
- Accept All Ideas and Viewpoints
- Encourage Imagination, Speculation, Questioning
- Develop Synthesis as a Thinking Process

9-10

TEACHING CRITICAL THINKING

- Emphasize Thought Processes
- Teach for Meaning
- Ask Thought-Provoking Questions
- Explain Your Thought Processes
- Students Explain Their Thought Processes
- Use Think-Aloud Strategies
- Summarize Main Ideas
- Be Consistent and Patient

9-11

ONE THINKING PROCESS

- **METACOGNITION**

  Awareness of One's Own Thinking Processes

9-12

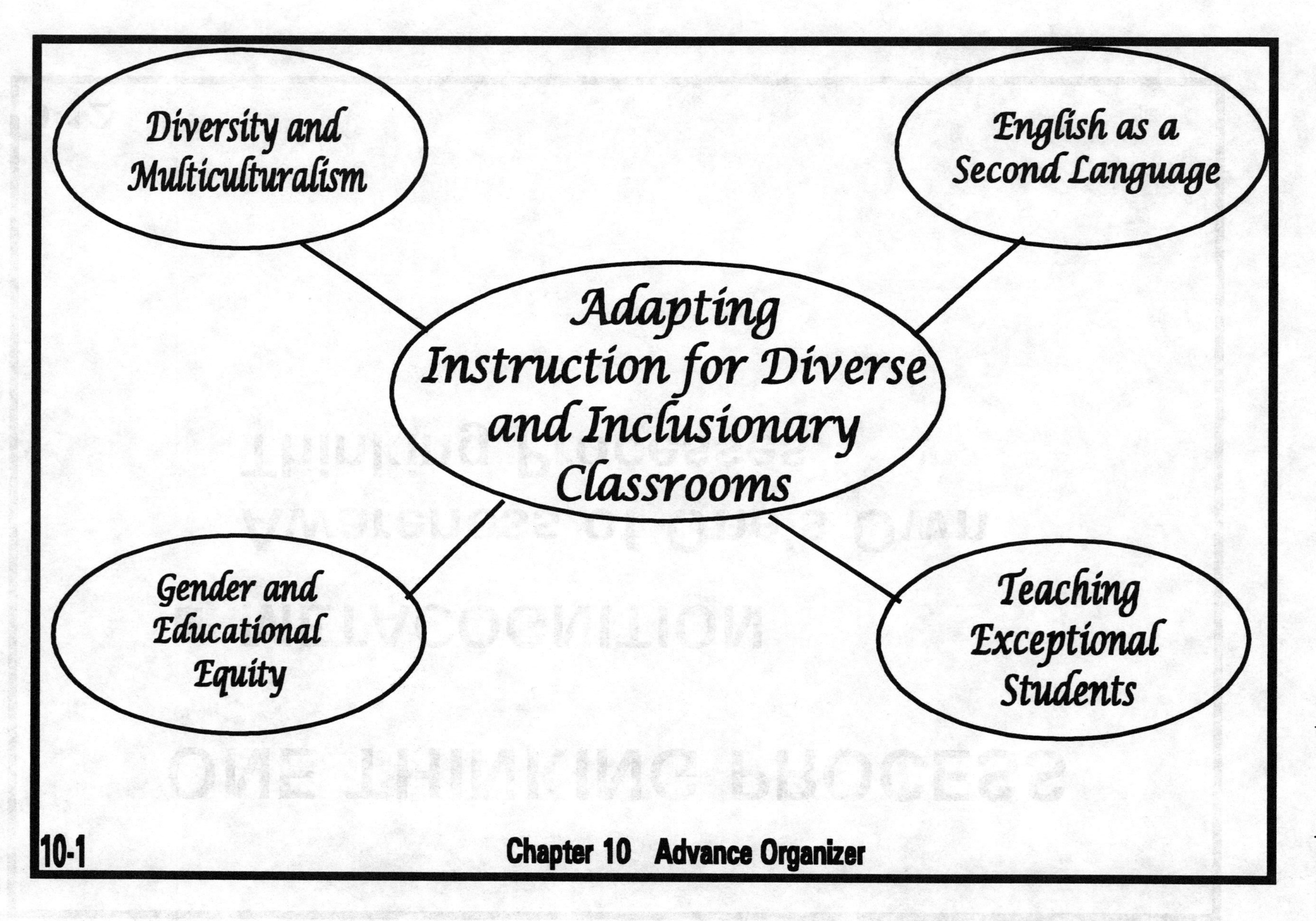
Diversity and Multiculturalism
English as a Second Language
Adapting Instruction for Diverse and Inclusionary Classrooms
Gender and Educational Equity
Teaching Exceptional Students
10-1
Chapter 10 Advance Organizer

MULTICULTURALISM EQUALS DIVERSITY IN:

- Ethnicity/Culture
- Race
- Language
- Religion/Beliefs
- Geographic Region or Community
- Physical Attributes
- Economics/Social Status

10-2

ESL

- LANGUAGE DIVERSITY
- LANGUAGE IMMERSION
- BILINGUAL EDUCATION

10-3

EXCEPTIONAL STUDENTS

- The Definitions
- The Laws
- The Instructional Adaptations

10-4

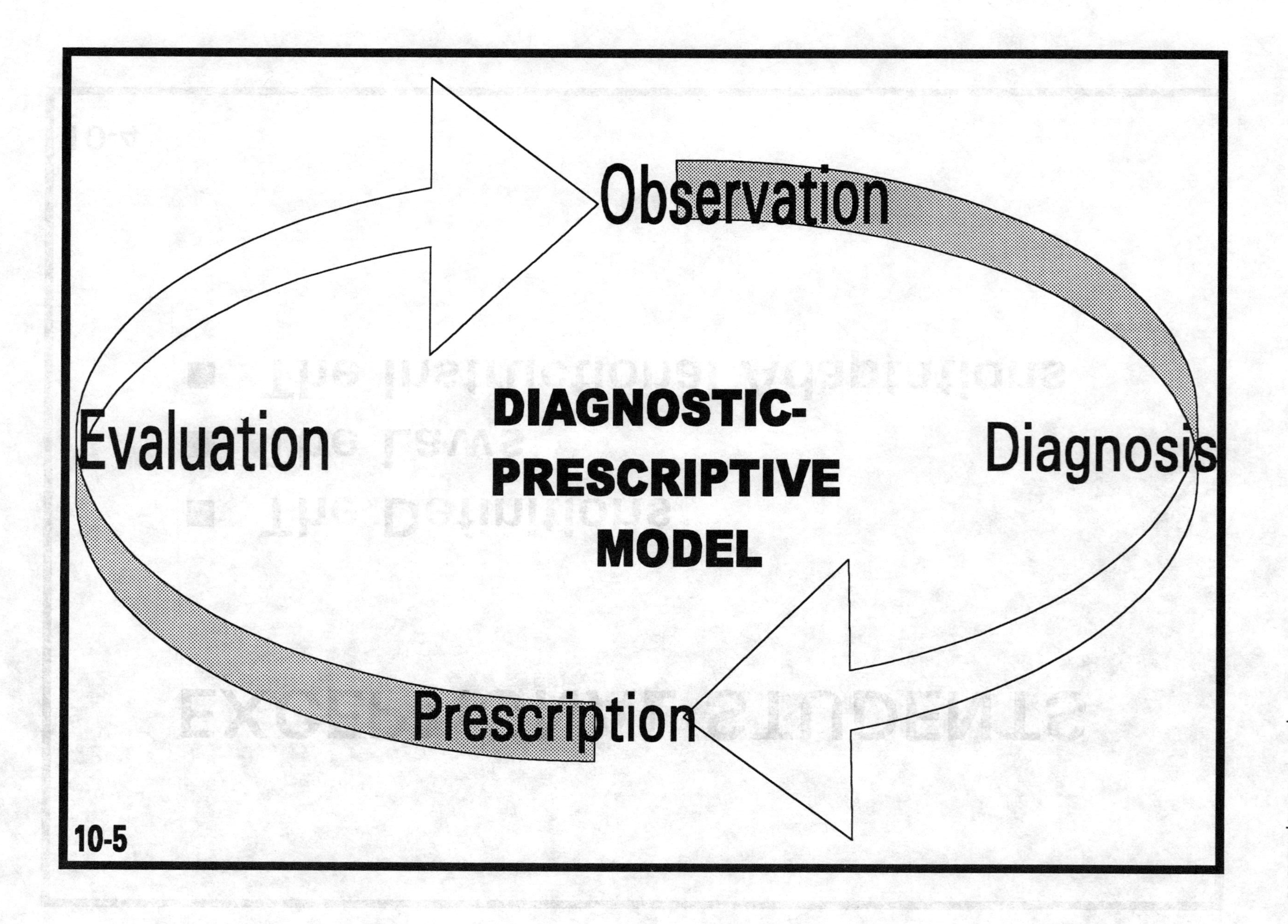
Observation
Evaluation
DIAGNOSTIC-
PRESCRIPTIVE
MODEL
Diagnosis
Prescription
10-5

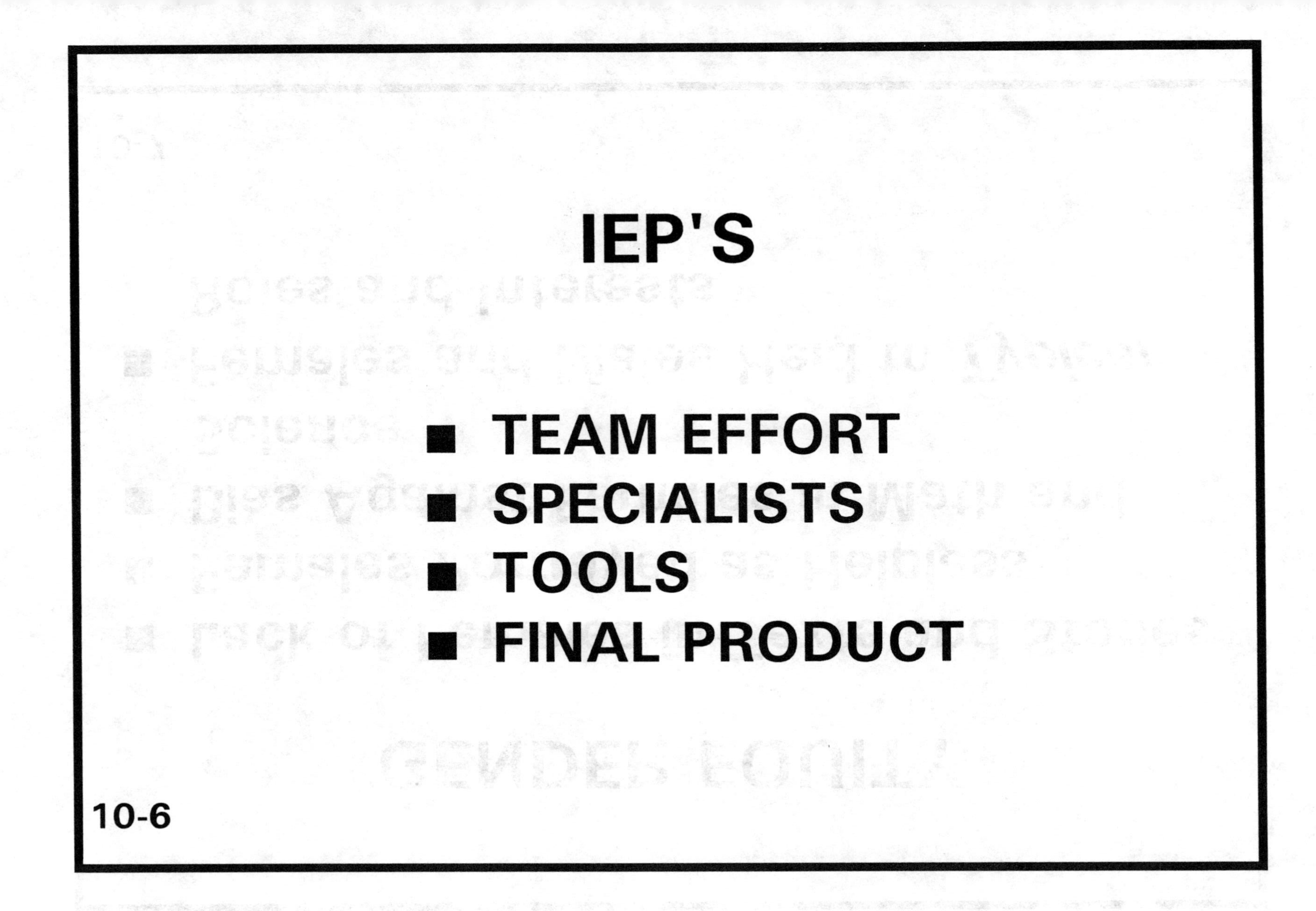
IEP'S
■ TEAM EFFORT
■ SPECIALISTS
■ TOOLS
■ FINAL PRODUCT
10-6

GENDER EQUITY

- Lack of Females in Texts and Stories
- Females Portrayed as Helpless
- Bias Against Females in Math and Science
- Females and Males Held to *Typical* Roles and Interests

10-7

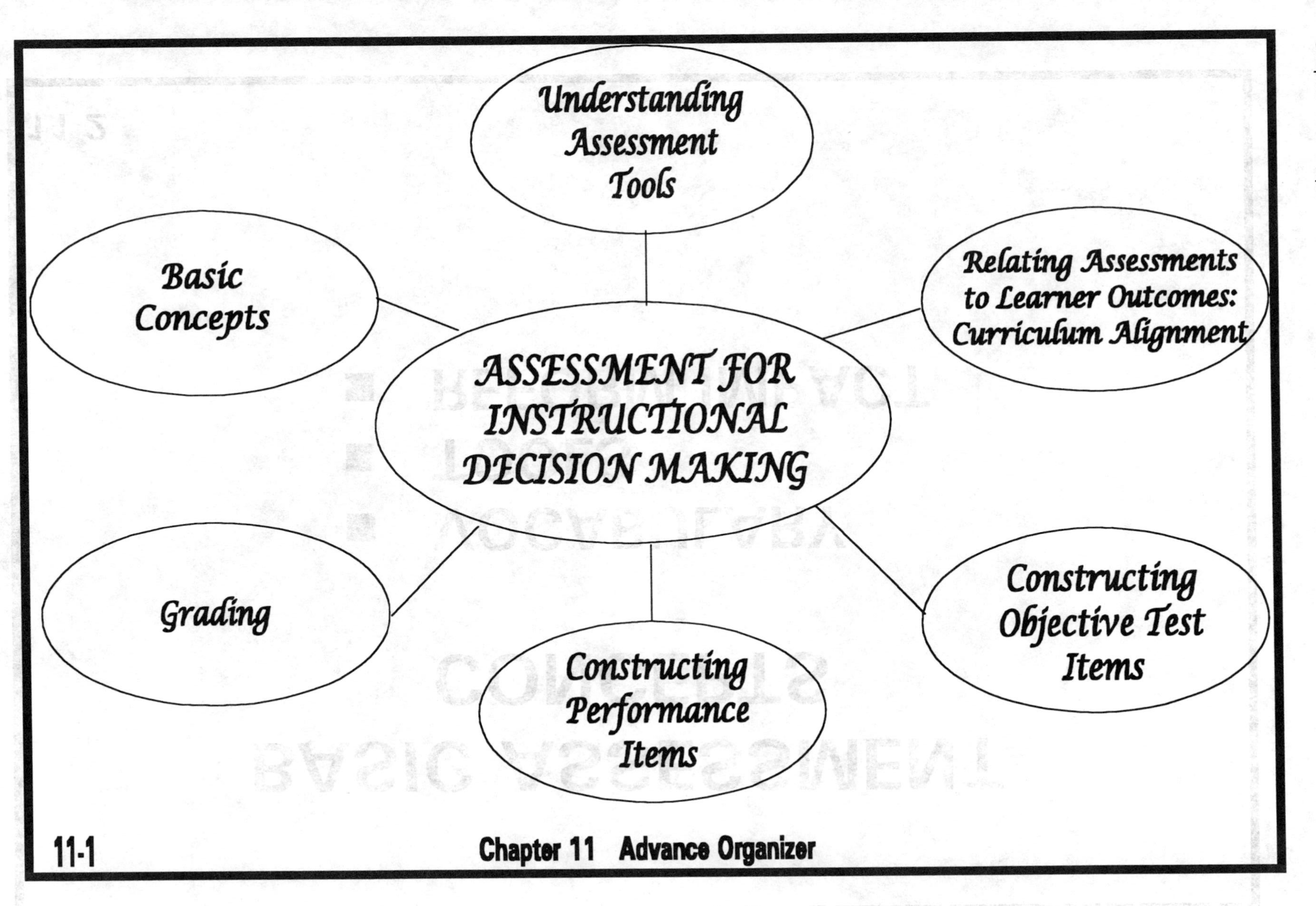

11-1 Chapter 11 Advance Organizer

BASIC ASSESSMENT CONCEPTS

- VOCABULARY
- TOOLS
- REFORM IMPACT

11-2

ASSESSMENT TOOLS

- STANDARDIZED TESTS
- TEACHER-MADE TESTS

11-3

CURRICULUM ALIGNMENT

- UNIT TESTS
- ACTIVITIES
- QUESTIONS
- TASKS

11-4

CONSTRUCTING TEST ITEMS

- TRUE-FALSE
- MATCHING
- SHORT ANSWER
- MULTIPLE CHOICE
- INTERPRETIVE EXERCISES

11-5

CONSTRUCTING PERFORMANCE ITEMS

- ESSAY QUESTIONS
- PERFORMANCE ASSESSMENTS
  - Rating Scales
  - Anecdotal Records
  - Portfolios
  - Rubrics

11-6

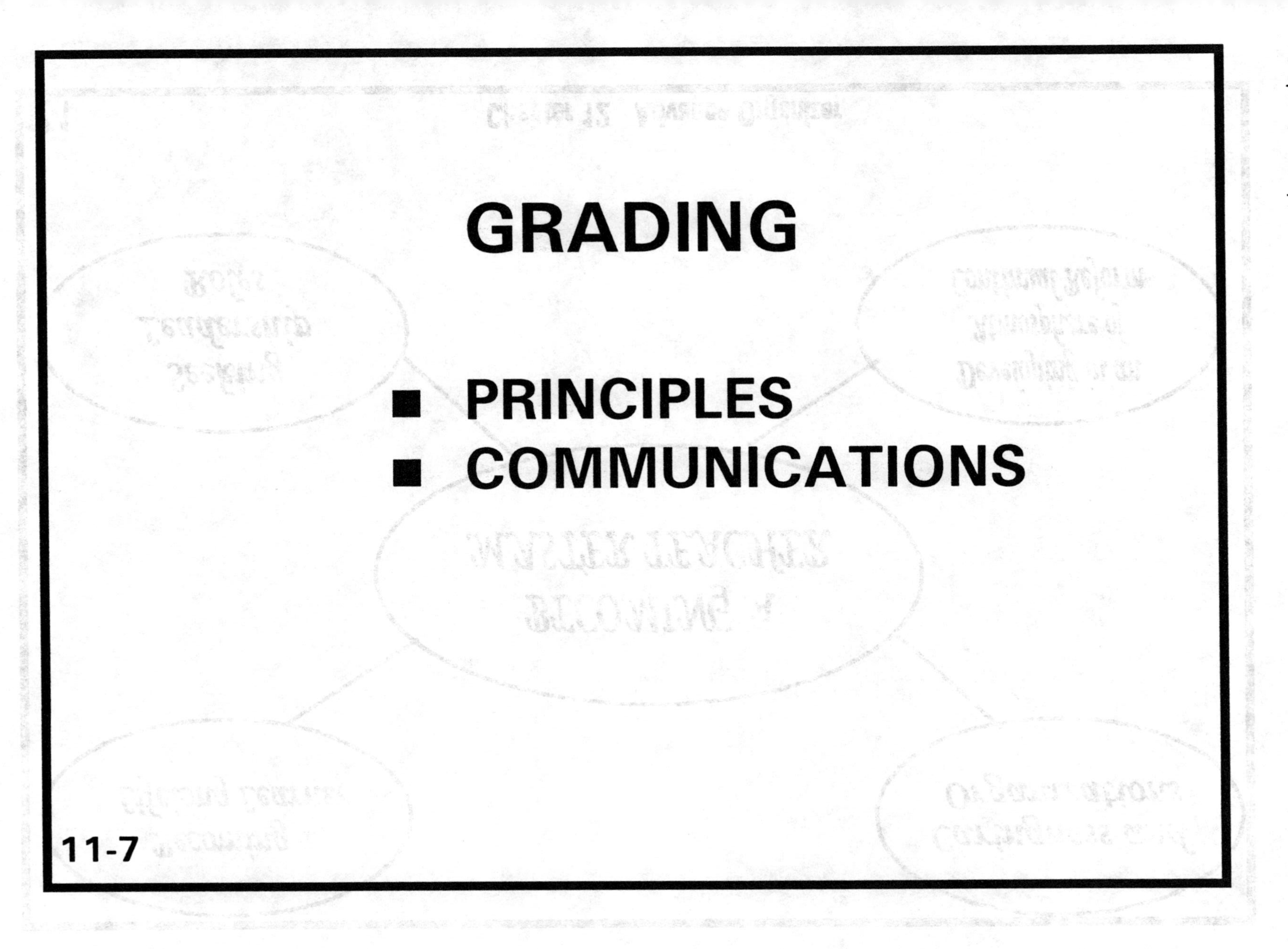
GRADING
■ PRINCIPLES
■ COMMUNICATIONS
11-7

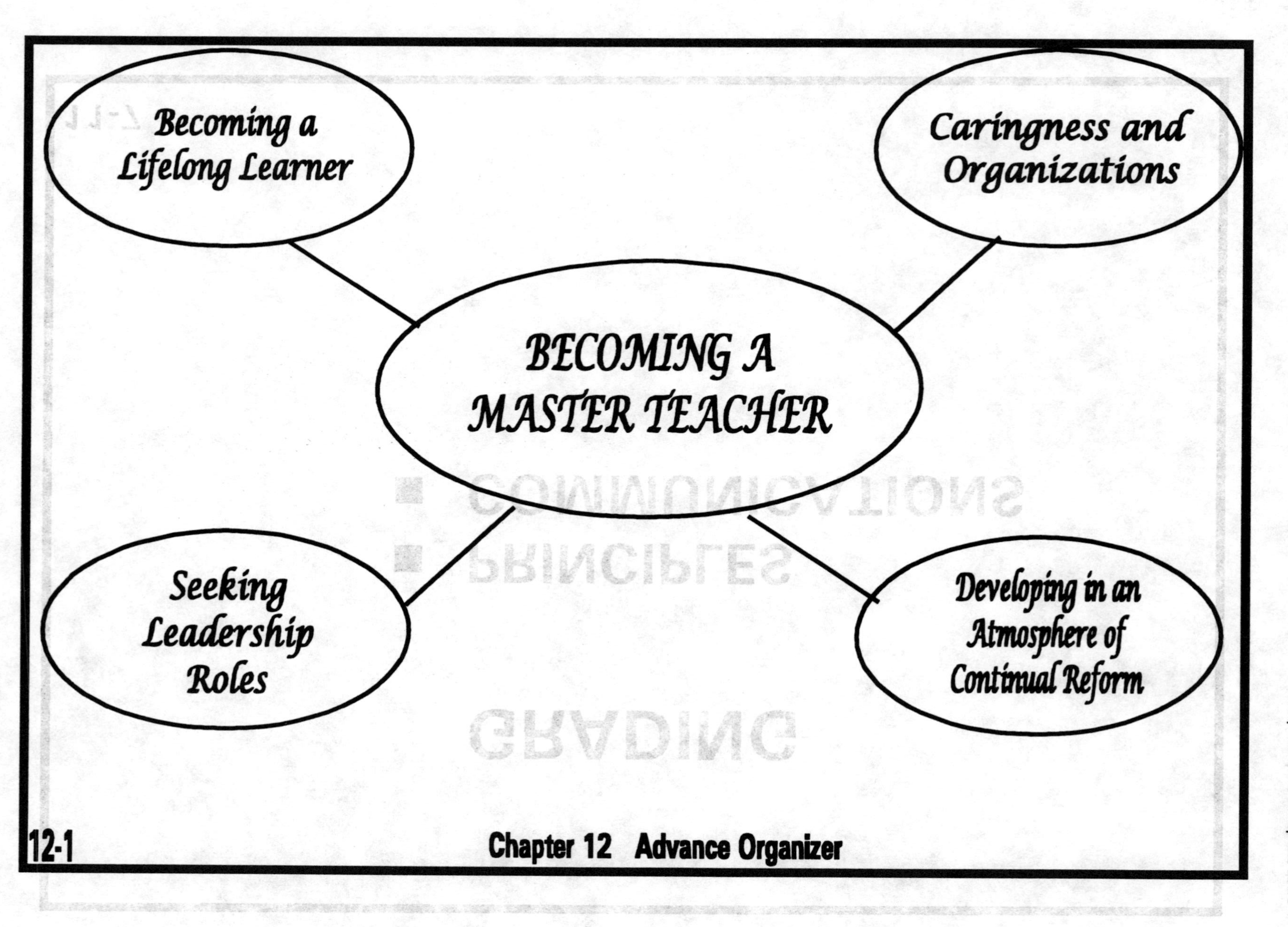
Becoming a Lifelong Learner
Caringness and Organizations
BECOMING A MASTER TEACHER
Seeking Leadership Roles
Developing in an Atmosphere of Continual Reform
12-1
Chapter 12 Advance Organizer

LIFELONG LEARNING

- Professional Plans and Growth
- Personal Growth
- Adult Learning Model

12-2

STAFF DEVELOPMENT

- Functions
- Perspectives
- Partnerships
- Never-ending Learning

12-3

REFORM ATMOSPHERE

- Effective Schools
- CBAM Model
- Knowledge Advancement

12-4

BEING A LEADER

- Personal Goals
- Career Preparation
- Master Teacher

12-5